Praise

Andy's first book, ███████████████ is a deep dive into ███████ ██████ Christ follower, a loving husband and father, a generous artist, and a man after God's own heart.

ANNIE F. DOWNS
New York Times bestselling author of *That Sounds Fun*

Andrew Osenga explores something many Christians feel but don't know how to articulate: the hunger for something older and truer than spiritual performance. This book doesn't scold or sell—it listens, laments, and then leads us back to what we've almost lost.

RUSSELL MOORE
Editor-in-Chief of *Christianity Today*

What Andrew has done here is timely and wise. These reflections will land softly and firmly in a cultural moment that is thirsty for the kind of invitation and guidance offered in *How to Remember*. It is a beautiful work, beautifully written that moves a reader from the chaos and turbulence of our shared cultural moment and toward a place of peace in their own chests.

JUSTIN MCROBERTS
Author of *Sacred Strides*; coauthor with Scott Erickson of *In the Low, May It Be So*, and *Prayer*; host of the *At Sea* podcast

It's not lost on me that the man from Normal, Illinois, the same person who would start a band called The Normals, would write such a wonderfully wise and out of the norm book on a very normal thing: being human. In a world that has turned the meaning of being human into a tireless race to procure comfort, Andrew reminds us that the marathon of life is just as much light, satisfying and beautiful as it is heavy, confusing and, even sometimes, unbearable. And like the friend that Andrew is, he doesn't run from the latter but instead, through his own vulnerability, shows us a way forward that embraces the whole of our humanity, bruises and all, with a curiosity for what was and a hopefulness for what is to come. There is an undeniable rhythm and melody to his words that, rest assured, I will be humming for many years to come. Thank you, my friend.

ZACH BOLEN
Writer and frontman for the band Citizens

HOW TO REMEMBER

FORGOTTEN PATHWAYS TO AN AUTHENTIC FAITH

Andrew Osenga

MOODY PUBLISHERS
CHICAGO

© 2025 by
ANDREW OSENGA

All rights reserved. No part of this book may be reproduced in any form without permission in writing from the publisher, except in the case of brief quotations embodied in critical articles or reviews.

All Scripture quotations, unless otherwise indicated, are taken from the Holy Bible, New International Version®, NIV®. Copyright ©1973, 1978, 1984, 2011 by Biblica, Inc.™ Used by permission of Zondervan. All rights reserved worldwide. www.zondervan.com The "NIV" and "New International Version" are trademarks registered in the United States Patent and Trademark Office by Biblica, Inc.™

Scripture quotations marked (ESV) are from the ESV® Bible (The Holy Bible, English Standard Version®), © 2001 by Crossway, a publishing ministry of Good News Publishers. Used by permission. All rights reserved. The ESV text may not be quoted in any publication made available to the public by a Creative Commons license. The ESV may not be translated in whole or in part into any other language.

Edited by Pamela Joy Pugh
Interior design: Koko Toyama
Cover design: Graham Terry
Cover images of canyon, dunes, and rock formation and courtesy of Freepik.
Author photo: Jeremy Cowart

ISBN: 978-0-8024-3533-0

Originally delivered by fleets of horse-drawn wagons, the affordable paperbacks from D. L. Moody's publishing house resourced the church and served everyday people. Now, after more than 125 years of publishing and ministry, Moody Publishers' mission remains the same—even if our delivery systems have changed a bit. For more information on other books (and resources) created from a biblical perspective, go to www.moodypublishers.com or write to:

Moody Publishers
820 N. LaSalle Boulevard
Chicago, IL 60610

1 3 5 7 9 10 8 6 4 2

Printed in the United States of America

To my daughters,

may whatever paths God sets before you lead you to beautiful places

Contents

1. The Oak Tree — 9
2. The Gift Shop — 13

ENOUGH — 17

3. The Van — 19
4. The Hymnals — 23

WHAT I FOUND — 27

5. Suffering (Songs of Lament) — 29
6. Doubt — 35
7. Time — 41
8. Place — 47
9. Faithfulness — 51
10. Joy — 57
11. Peace — 63
12. I Need to Hear You (A Digression) — 69

THE MYSTERIES — 73

13. Presence — 75
14. Glory — 81
15. Righteousness and Justice — 85
16. Mercy — 91
17. Forgiveness — 95
18. Otherness — 101

HONORABLE MENTIONS — 107

19. Songs of Exodus — 109
20. Stories of Jesus — 115
21. Songs of Scripture — 119

MARROW — 123

22. Liturgies (A Digression) — 125
23. The Lessons — 127
24. Prayers in the Airport — 131
25. Confession / Absolution — 137
26. Creeds — 143
27. Play the Rests (Quiet Together) — 149
28. Postures — 155
29. Symbols — 159

GARDEN — 163

30. The Quiet Hours — 165
31. Guided Prayer — 171
32. Sacred Spaces — 177
33. Coloring on the Wall — 183
34. Generations — 187
35. Others — 193
36. Grieving — 197
37. Walking — 203
38. Trees — 207

Thank You — 209
Notes — 211

1.

The Oak Tree

ON A SUNNY MONDAY AFTERNOON one autumn, I stepped out of a meeting to find a slew of texts and phone calls from my family. One of the giant sixty-year-old oaks behind our house had suddenly splintered, sending half the tree crashing down on the fence that separated our yard from our neighbor's.

What we found in the fallen branches was surprising. A deep, dark discoloration was running through the middle of each section, both of what was on the ground and the rest of the tree still standing.

Though the oak appeared full and vibrant and healthy, it was actually deeply diseased and rotting from the inside out. We discovered the same dark rings in the other three trees in our yard, so the rot was likely spreading across our neighborhood.

What if all the big, old, trustworthy trees around us suddenly fall or need to be taken down? It will change so much of what we know and love about our street and our homes. It will be sad, but there will also be space for new trees to grow and eventually become the big, old, trustworthy trees for the next generation of families who live here on this street.

Something about this seemed familiar.

I'm a church kid. I grew up in a Christian family who went to church *all* the time. My parents were, and still are, a part of nearly every committee, group, and project going on in the building.

So much of who I am and what I care about was formed from my childhood experiences there. That's where I learned about Jesus and caring for others, became familiar with the classic hymns, and met a bunch of people who thought those things mattered and tried to live their lives in a way that reflected that.

Now I've spent over half of my life in "Christian" work.

I signed a record deal the day I turned nineteen, dropped out of college, and went on tour with my first band, The Normals. Over the next twenty-five years I would also become a member of a fairly popular Christian band named Caedmon's Call, and a touring guitar player for many artists in Christian music, such as Andrew Peterson, Steven Curtis Chapman, and Jars of Clay. Somehow, I ended up in A&R (working directly with artists and their songs) at two of the biggest record companies in Christian music, working with a large number of the artists and songwriters in that industry and discovering and developing some who have become quite successful.

As a songwriter myself, I've released many albums, played hundreds of my own concerts, and had my songs recorded by many well-known artists; I've also sung at worship services around the world.

I say all that only to tell you of the experiences that have led to this book. I won't include any more name-droppy paragraphs like the last two in the rest of these pages, I promise. The point is, I've seen many different types of churches, leaders, and communities and have been deeply impacted by the many amazing ways God is working.

But I've also seen a lot of fallen branches. People who have left the church, sometimes quietly, sometimes angrily. More often than we might realize, what has looked so vibrant and alive from the outside has a sickness running through it.

Leaders get caught in scandals, pastors are exposed as narcissists, politics takes priority over the gospel, churches' desires to grow leave the people in the seats feeling like numbers rather than individuals. Behind it all is a uniquely Western drive to make everything bigger and faster and more efficient, sometimes hiding a landscape of pollution and inequity in its shadow.

I don't think we are aware of how much the world around us has shaped our assumptions of value, economy, and cause and effect. Just as some babies are born with blue eyes and some with brown, I believe many of us are capitalist children, born with eyes that see the world as status to achieve, products to sell, or products to consume.

This is not our fault, yet part of the process of maturity is recognizing this natural bias and working to reorganize our lives along priorities of our own choosing.

If American consumerism has shaped how we see the world, then, obviously, it will have shaped the American church as well.

Some of the more positive ways this worldview has impacted the church has allowed its message to spread around the planet, in ways and forms never before seen, at a scale previously unimaginable. Of course, to achieve that reach, what gets communicated must be simplified to its lowest common denominator, taking much of its nuance, beauty, and contemplation—things that would be dear and familiar to Christians before us—and leaving it behind.

The ways of Jesus, a disciple must eventually learn, involve quite a lot of nuance, beauty, and contemplation.

I fear that, in order to grow faster, we have cut ourselves off from our roots, and now we are surprised that our plants are withering.

This is how we find ourselves with an American church full of failing leaders, shrinking numbers, and little knowledge about its own history.

Are we surprised, then, when more and more branches start falling from the trees?

2.

The Gift Shop

COULD IT BE THAT PEOPLE coming to church in search of God, healing, and community are instead finding celebrity pastors and the worship band's latest single—so they're turning around and heading back out?

When the Jesus who told us to love our neighbor and turn the other cheek is now being used as a bumper sticker to "take our country back for God," are we surprised that people in grief and pain aren't finding the peace and freedom they are seeking?

But the good news, and it is so good, is that Jesus is not even a little bit done with the church, nor is He even a little bit scared of any of these things that keep some of us up all night.

You and I have been invited into a friendship with God in a holy and mysterious way, beyond our own power. He who began it will be faithful to complete it.

I have a lot of friends who have left the church over the years. Some of them still stay away, but a few have started to come back. They miss the community, the sense of collective purpose. They miss feeling close to God and serving those around them. They have kids now and they want their kids to learn about Jesus and have shared experiences with other young believers.

So, I'm not surprised every time I see another friend show up at our small Anglican church, where the service may seem, on the surface, kind of rote and there's not a screen in sight. Or I hear they're joining up with a house church in their neighborhood or going back to the small and established AME church down by the park.

They don't want the celebrity pastor. They don't want fog machines and light shows. They want people to know their names and to notice when they're not there. They want to belong and be known.

Isn't that what we all want? To be seen, to be known and, ultimately, to be loved?

(And please know that I've got nothing at all against a giant church with eight services and a telecast pastor. I have seen how God uses them, ministering both to their congregations and in their communities. Yet it's so hard for individuals to be seen or known in a large place like that. So easy to feel lost in the crowd. That's an uphill battle for everyone involved, as thoughtful and well-meaning as I know many of those pastors and churches to be.)

At its furthest extreme, these churches can feel like one more "product" to be sold. One of the great challenges of the contemporary church is that, at times, we're handed our faith-to-go like we're rushing by a drive-thru, rather than hunting, gathering, prepping, cooking, and finally feasting on the fruits of our labors. We eat it so fast that we don't savor it, nor do we really understand where it's come from.

As capitalism has commodified the Christian experience, it has also unwittingly filtered out the parts that were too challenging, too boring, or too controversial to pass along as product. But the challenging parts and the not-exciting parts and the controversial parts are, well ...

... those are a huge part of Christianity.

Following Jesus has been, since the very beginning, a countercultural way of living. It was never meant to sit on a bookstore shelf. It is a revolution in the wake of a resurrection.

It's like we've spent years in a gift shop for the Grand Canyon. We've been wearing the T-shirts, learning the history, and setting up imaginary worlds with the figurines ... until suddenly something catches our eye. We realize that there's a little light poking through a shuttered-up window. As we tear down the blinds, we are startled to realize that we've been next to the Canyon itself the whole time.

This might be thrilling and it might even be a bit scary. You might make a mess in your haste to get out of the gift shop. (For your mother or your pastor watching from afar, it might be scary as well.)

But when you know the Grand Canyon is out there, you're not going to stay inside.

For thousands of years, Christians have been driven by a spiritual hunger to explore the beauty and the wildness and the neverending richness of God. And the bottom line is that we're the same as those who came before us. Searching like explorers, we have to keep looking deeper, finding the hidden and humble paths to the divine presence we feel beyond our senses. Thankfully, many of these earlier explorers, our spiritual ancestors, have left us a rich legacy of what they've found.

Just as we have new trees taking root in our yard, we are seeing new signs of life in the church in America. More and more, contemporary Christians are looking to find things about the church they can trust. They are putting down roots in well-seasoned soil and finding there the legacy of overlooked songs, prayers, and practices to guide them into a sacred and intimate life with Jesus.

What follows are a series of short essays on some of what I've learned about these forgotten songs, prayers, and practices of believers who have gone before us. Our culture has raced past these older guideposts in its haste to grow and stay relevant, because we've forgotten that relevance is not about being trendy and modern. To be relevant is simply to be trustworthy to those who need you.

There is infinitely more to discover about each of these ideas, to be very clear. If what I'm discussing is new to you, know that this is simply to serve as an introduction. If the topic is familiar, I hope I can offer a new way to look at it.

It's my hope and prayer that some of the practices and ideas you find in this book (none of which are my invention, nor my discovery) can help guide you into a richer, deeper, and more satisfying life with the Jesus who loves you so much more than you can possibly imagine.

ENOUGH

What we sing matters.
The words we speak matter.
The way we live matters.

We are giving ourselves a vocabulary.
We are teaching the language of the Christian life,
to ourselves, to our children, and to the world around us.

It's a life that gives us enough . . .

enough to bear suffering and doubt.
enough to taste and celebrate joy.
enough to rest in plenty or in need,
to walk together or alone.

for we know we are never alone.

It's a life that might have enemies,
and that is willing to love them,
because we are held and formed,
at all times,
in all ways,
by Jesus.

3.

The Van

MOST PEOPLE MY AGE WERE going back for their sophomore year in college when my bandmates and I headed off on our first tour. We would end up putting 300,000 miles on that 15-passenger van over the next four and a half years, playing every state in "the lower 48."

It was the late nineties and Christian music youth group culture was at its height. Every church in every town was bringing bands in for lock-ins and youth rallies, and I'm pretty sure we played them all.

I could not have known what a gift this would be for my young and sheltered faith.

While other nineteen-year-olds were taking their Religions of the World class, I was building new friendships around the country every day with Baptists, Lutherans, Presbyterians, Non-denoms, Apostolics, Catholics, and more. You name it.

Before I understood what the differences in their theologies were, I understood that they were people who really loved Jesus, and who were dearly loved by Him.

Where I once, as a child, had assumed that all Christians were Christians like I was a Christian, with the same songs and traditions and church practices, I was suddenly aware that followers of Jesus came in many flavors. I began to learn what separated my friends from one another and heard some claim that one preference was right, and the others were wrong—yet I could not unlearn what I knew to be true: My friends' faith was genuine.

Some of these differences seemed surface level, like how people dressed or what style of service they held. (I now realize those are not surface distinctions at all, by the way.) Then there were the theological variations. Some were minor, some major. For the most part, though, there was a core belief in Jesus, His death and resurrection.

Years later, when I was a young father, two of my daughters attended a Spanish immersion school. Starting on the first day of kindergarten, the teachers spoke naturally in Spanish, without translation. The kids were so young that they were still learning English at that point, and they quickly picked up the second language and were basically conversational by the end of first grade.

My early years of musical traveling were similar. I absorbed the wildly various expressions of faith I encountered without explanation, only parsing their differences after already experiencing their beauty and value.

Having grown up in a fundamentalist church in a cornfield in Illinois, I had a narrow view of Christianity and the lifestyle that surrounded it. I knew some Baptist and Methodist hymns, some Maranatha praise choruses, and some eighties and nineties contemporary Christian music (that is, CCM). I knew about baby dedications and altar calls, what companies to boycott, and all the things good Christians didn't do.

All of a sudden, I was being exposed to concepts like *liturgies* and *creeds*. I was hearing people read Scripture together out loud. People were standing and kneeling (and standing and kneeling and standing and kneeling) and randomly touching their heads and chests. Some people would pray together in a short song they all knew, praising God from whom all blessings flow. Other people were dancing with flags, while others were freestyling on the Hammond organ. They took Communion every month, or every week. Sometimes even from the same cup. At some places the wine was actually wine! *The scandal!*

There were people who were generally quiet. And those who were very much not. There were rooms as solemn as a whisper that made you feel small and thoughtful, while others that made you feel like you were a part of the bustle of their city, the hands and feet of Jesus in action.

Meanwhile, as my relationships deepened, the city of Nashville was slowly becoming my own, and I began to gingerly invest myself and my heart into the community I found there, something that still felt unnatural to this sensitive kid from the Illinois cornfield.

Eventually, I fell into a group of other college-age musicians, led by a book-collecting, guitar-playing Presbyterian pastor. Kevin taught us reformed theology at his weekly Bible studies and recruited us to help him write and record new music for forgotten old hymn lyrics in his spare time. (We, being mostly single, barely employed musicians, had more than enough of our own spare time in those days.)

Kevin would tell us the stories of the hymnwriters and what led to their songs, both songs we knew and songs we'd never heard of. We learned how music and theology used to be taught together, which is why many renowned pastors also wrote their own hymns, such as John Calvin, George Whitefield, Martin Luther, Charles Spurgeon, and John Newton.

As a music lover, I'll be honest and say that some of the hymns felt more like sermon notes than great songs, as sometimes poetry was sacrificed on the altar of information and doctrine. Still, like any genre, the best rises to the top, and when it comes to hymns, the cup runs over with all the greatness. I found a staggering and surprising wealth of amazing songs to discover.

Our little crew were sponges, soaking up all the truly inspiring old hymns Kevin was introducing to us. Not just the hymns in isolation, either, but what was behind their form and structure. A song written specifically and intentionally to be sung together is different from a pop song we sing along with. I'd never realized the distinction before.

In fact, between what I was learning with my friends in Nashville and absorbing from the churches of my friends across the country, there was *so* much I'd never realized.

About songs, yes, but much more so about the faith at the heart of the songs themselves.

4.

The Hymnals

I CLOSE MY EYES AND see a snapshot of a memory of my old country church as the sun sets over the cornfields.

My dad was the choir director, and my mom the piano player. We had Sunday night church because all good Christians have Sunday night church (or at least they did in the eighties), and every now and then one of those nights would be a "hymn night." It was usually a bunch of old people and my parents—and me and my brother, bored in a very hard pew, passing notes back and forth.

The old folks would take turns calling out a number, my mom would turn to that page, she'd start to play, and we would sing that song. Then we'd do the next song. For exactly sixty minutes, and then we could go home.

Now years later, I go back to those old songs more and more and realize that what we had been singing—messages of grace and beauty and longing and redemption—didn't always line up with what was being preached: lists of all the things that good Christians didn't do.

Hidden there in those old red hymnals, God was sneaking messages to a bored little kid who would one day really need to have heard them.

As I started to think about it, these were some of these same sacred songs being sung at almost every one of these churches I had been traveling to over the years, and some of them sit under far corners of the same big tent of belief. How fascinating is this?

Is something deeper happening in these songs? Something that gets communicated beyond lyric and rhyme, in the way that God intertwines melody and memory, that allows songs to move around like spies between camps?

I had gotten curious, so I started to look through my old hymnbooks.

Oh yeah, I have an accidental hymnal collection.

Many churches don't use hymnals anymore, so often when I would visit a place, I'd find myself backstage packing up my guitar next to stacks of boxes of these forgotten old books. Sometimes they would just sort of call out to me, and I'd ask if I could have one. "Take them all!" would be the usual reply.

Now I find myself with a hundred or more of these old hymnals. I'd never really spent much time with them, until a few years ago when some friends and I started to gather to try and write new communal songs in this same tradition. Leading Anchor Hymns, as this community was eventually named, has become a big part of the past few years of my life, and a big part of that work involves looking for forgotten hymn lyrics that we can use as inspiration for fresh new songs.

Once I'd started digging through the collection, I realized it was a lot more varied than I'd expected.

For all the songs that have lasted through the ages, a great many of them have not. And for good reason. Some are just bad songs;

some are nationalist or racist (let's keep moving, please) and those deserve to be forgotten.

Many are very particular to a denomination in a certain time, and we could probably all learn from these guys. The mid-twentieth century Baptists talk a lot about obedience and repentance. Lutherans in the sixties and seventies talk a lot about serving the community and the beauty of creation. The old spirituals sing about freedom, long-suffering, and heaven. In fact, all the hymns from the Great Depression talk about heaven, in any denomination. The Presbyterians sing that the way you *think* about God matters. We can learn a lot from all these unique eras of different groups.

Then there are the classics, the forty or fifty songs found in every single one of these hymnals: "Amazing Grace." "How Great Thou Art." "Great Is Thy Faithfulness."

These are the songs sung by both the most hardcore fundamentalist and the most radical liberal. They're sung at the gravesides of the most casually religious and also the deepest believer.

Why?

I started my own unscientific, college dropout–level research. I printed out the lyrics of each of those familiar hymns and looked for what was common among them.

My hunch was that there was something buried in those words, and their melodies, that spoke to a shared humanity, deeper even than our theology or our religiosity.

WHAT I FOUND

Here's what I found:
1. An honesty about suffering and doubt.
2. An awareness of time and place.
3. God's faithfulness—in joy, in spiritual intimacy, in suffering and in doubt, at all times, everywhere.
4. God's mysterious majesty—His presence, His glory, His goodness, and His otherness.

These themes were present in virtually all of the songs that transcended era and denomination.

Here's the crazier thing: After two decades of work in worship music, I have found that these themes are often absent in many, *though by no means all*, of our worship music today.

I want to explore the songs it seems we may have forgotten. And to dig deeper, beneath the songs themselves, into the themes and ideas that could teach us and shape us, if we would learn to sing them again.

5.

Suffering

SONGS OF LAMENT

Be still, my soul; when dearest friends depart,
and all is darkened in the vale of tears,
then shalt thou better know His love, His heart,
who comes to soothe thy sorrow and thy fears.

— "BE STILL, MY SOUL," KATHRINA VON SCHLEGEL, 1752

MANY YEARS AGO, I SPENT some time in India, traveling to various cities, recording local musicians, and writing songs based on the stories I was encountering. It was a wild and life-changing trip, due both to the beauty of the nation and its music, and also its overwhelming oppression and poverty.

Almost everywhere you looked, the streets were lined with cardboard houses and homeless children, victims of the cruel caste system. The people were beautiful, but the sight was heartbreaking, the filth overwhelming, and the noise constant. Nothing can prepare you for sleepless nights in a five-star hotel overlooking a slum where children are playing and living in a pile of trash outside your window.

How to Remember

At one point during our trip, Colin Powell (at that time the US Secretary of State) was coming to Mumbai for a visit. All of a sudden, certain streets were eerily quiet. Crisp and beautiful. Not a beggar to be seen.

All along the path from the airport to the place where Powell would be staying, to the palace he'd be visiting and back, giant white walls had been erected. The roads had been cleaned and fresh grass laid down, so that the general's experience of India would be one of serene beauty, while on the other side of the walls lived the heaving throngs of chaos that marked the familiar Indian streets.

My hunch is that General Powell was not fooled by the ruse. Surely, his Indian escorts weren't either, though maybe, for a minute, looking down those clean, safe streets, they might almost wish they could be.

If so, I would understand. I know that feeling.

My own life has been deeply marked by suffering, and there are many ways I've tried to put up my own white walls and keep myself from the truth of my own pain and sadness.

But those walls in India didn't address the oppression of the caste system or feed the hungry children, it just hid them from view. Just as hiding from my own loneliness or sadness only made me more miserable and unable to ask anyone for help. It was a spiral that could have had no end, were it not for the kindness of God, caring for me through the loving, pursuing friendships of my community (often when I was not the most eager recipient).

If you're old enough to read this sentence, then I imagine you've probably suffered in some way too.

There are things we deeply long for that we may never have. Partners. Children. Career. We've lost family and friends too soon. We are plagued by chronic pain, disease, crushing financial burdens, the hidden worlds of abuse and addiction. The broken relationships that refuse to heal no matter what we do.

Suffering is by no means the only prerequisite of being human, but it is surely one of them.

For most of human history, this was an undeniable fact. A general understanding of life. However, our culture has these unique blessings—painkillers, cellphones, air conditioning, grocery stores, airplanes—which are also in a strange way curses, in that they put cushioning barriers between us and the raw reality of being human. They allow us to live an illusion that suffering is abnormal and out of the ordinary.

Have you felt this mentality even creep into our Sunday morning songs at times? This unstated idea that because God cares about our lives, they should also be painless. I know I have. It sets us up for constant disillusionment, doesn't it?

Yet I continue to be amazed by this:

That Jesus became human is the most shocking thing about Christianity. And that He did not come as a conqueror or a king, but as a helpless child, who would go on to live as a refugee and a homeless man before being ultimately abandoned and tortured to death.

In fact, in the Bible we're introduced to Him like this:

> *He had no beauty or majesty to attract us to him, nothing in his appearance that we should desire him. He was despised and rejected by mankind, a man of suffering, and familiar with pain. Like one from whom people hide their faces he was despised, and we held him in low esteem. (Isa. 53:2–3)*

Talk about a first impression.

I'll be honest, there are days when it can be a little hard to be friends with people who seem like they've had a totally easy ride, whether or not this is true. I'm both jealous and confident that they couldn't really understand my life and the problems I've had.

Then other times you meet someone, and you know that they just "get it." You're able to connect and trust each other because you've both been through similar challenges.

This is where Christ meets us—in humility, eye to eye. "A man of sorrows," as some versions of Scripture call Him, who intentionally endured great pain to sit with us when we have no choice left but to be honest about what's really going on.

> *Abide with me: fast falls the eventide;*
> *the darkness deepens; Lord, with me abide.*
> *When other helpers fail and comforts flee,*
> *Help of the helpless, O abide with me.*
> —"ABIDE WITH ME," HENRY FRANCIS LYTE, 1847

Our pain is not scary for Jesus. It is not unwelcome or unholy. It is the most sacred and natural way to come before God.

Our deepest hurts and longings are the places closest to the heart of God. They are where we feel the brokenness and the awareness of the beauty of His creation. We feel the heartbreak and longing of our Creator when we muster the courage to look at those deepest hurts and longings and say, in an inverse echo of God Himself:

"It was good! It is not as good now as it should be, but it will be again!"

My friends, to not come honestly to God is to deny our humanity, and to deny His sacrificial act of meeting us there. The good news of Jesus is that He came for the broken and the sick. That was the whole point, after all.

And so, we bring our pain before Him, together as a church, in song. We cry out in our loss, grief, and anguish. Even our anger. We call these songs "laments."

Indeed, a book of the Bible is titled "Lamentations," an entire book full of songs of suffering.

One of the most famous songs of lament handed down within the past few generations is the hymn "It Is Well," written after a two-year span in which its author, Horatio Spafford, lost his four-year-old son to scarlet fever, his successful real estate business to the Great Chicago Fire, and then his four other children, all daughters, in a shipwreck.

> *When peace like a river attendeth my way,*
> *when sorrows like sea billows roll;*
> *whatever my lot, thou hast taught me to say,*
> *"It is well, it is well, with my soul."*
> —"IT IS WELL WITH MY SOUL," HORATIO SPAFFORD, 1873

You would think the song ends there, like the stages of grief, in acceptance, but no, the story isn't over. The next four verses actually move forward into themes of sin, redemption, and heaven. To sing of suffering does not mean you have to wallow in it and stay there forever. It simply means you are honest about where you are at the moment you are in it.

In some mysterious way, crying out to God, "Why have you abandoned me?!" has been for many the pathway to hope, and even, as impossible as it may seem, to joy.

If we try to take a shortcut and jump straight to the victory, as some churches (or radio stations) have chosen to do, we might find that we actually push away those of us who don't feel very victorious. (Which, you know, is most of us, most of the time.)

Stories without conflict aren't stories worth telling; that's why the best Batman movies have the most dangerous villains.

If we only play songs that are positive and encouraging, are we telling those who listen that their suffering is something that needs to be hidden, or to be ashamed of? Are we putting up white walls that hide our problems and actually keep us from bringing them before God?

A lot of the pain in my life is not mine alone, and I don't need to tell stories that aren't mine to tell, but I can tell you this: The *only* reason I still have a relationship with Jesus is that He was a man of suffering, well acquainted with grief.

Because I am too.

6.

Doubt

Just as I am, though tossed about
with many a conflict, many a doubt,
fightings and fears within, without,
O Lamb of God, I come, I come.
—"JUST AS I AM," CHARLOTTE ELLIOTT, 1836

I WOULD LOVE TO SEE a miracle.

I would love for something so wild and unexplainable to happen that my faith didn't have to be faith anymore.

I'd love to be healed. To fix all my problems and make the pain go away. To part the sea of my mortgage and medical bills and my mild to medium seasonal depression.

This has got to be why people were always flocking around Jesus, not because they wanted to love their enemies and lay down their lives in humility, but because they wanted to see what was going on. They wanted to see crazy things happen. They wanted to be healed.

Wouldn't we all be in that crowd?

I think if I was given the choice between making all that hurts or troubles me go away or actually seeing God very clearly in some undeniable, scientifically accountable, doubt-eliminating way, I would keep my pain and problems every time. I would know, then, for certain, how temporary they were, and how secure I really was.

We are not given that clarity, though. Instead, we are born with a coin in our hand with faith on one side and doubt on the other. Whichever face you choose to look at, the other is right there, gnawing into your palm.

That's good news for the doubter, and a thorn in the side of the faithful.

We don't like to think about it, however, and we really don't like to talk about it.

In my church culture growing up, doubting was viewed as sinful. An act of rebellion. Perhaps you've seen the movies where the atheist professors are finally converted by self-righteous culture warrior students who, yes, waver in their faith on their knees a little bit in the second act but emerge triumphant in the big classroom showdown finale.

America's for winners, after all. Big slogans. Short sentences. No fear. No doubt.

Doubting makes us feel weak and we don't like that. It doesn't give the best look or move products off the shelves. Well, we can't have that.

So we clench our fists and hide what's real, inadvertently giving what's not allowed to be spoken more power.

And yet for me, it was like those Sunday night hymn sings were sent as messages in bottles, floating in the ocean, waiting for their moment to be discovered, just when they were needed.

> *When darkness veils his lovely face,*
> *I rest on his unchanging grace.*
> —"MY HOPE IS BUILT ON NOTHING LESS," EDWARD MOTE, 1834

O Lord, haste the day when my faith shall be sight.
—"IT IS WELL WITH MY SOUL," HORATIO SPAFFORD, 1873

We walk by faith and not by sight,
no gracious words we hear
from Him who spoke as none e'er spoke,
but we believe Him near.

We may not touch His hands and side,
nor follow where He trod;
but in His promise we rejoice
and cry, "My Lord and God!"
—"WE WALK BY FAITH AND NOT BY SIGHT," HENRY ALFORD, 1844

It turns out, I grew up singing about doubt; I just didn't realize it.

Like the hero in those cheesy movies, after a much darker second act, Jesus did indeed emerge victorious at the finale. Victorious, but scarred.

He has actual holes in His hands. A giant wound still in His side.

When He visits His friends a little later, some are excited to see Him. Some are freaked out. I get that. The apostle John makes sure to tell us the story of his friend Thomas, who says he has to touch those wounds before accepting what others are telling him.

The friends wanted Jesus to stay with them, to be who and what they wanted Him to be.

And so . . . faith it was for them.

And faith it is for us.

And that means doubt. You simply can't have one without the other. Two sides of the same coin.

Faith is believing in what we can't see, even though what we want to see is Jesus in the flesh right here beside us. We don't get that, and yes, that is hard, but we are not left alone.

The same John who tells us about his friend Thomas also shares something Jesus said shortly before the crucifixion:

> *"But the Advocate [or Helper/Friend/Counselor], the Holy Spirit, whom the Father will send in my name, will teach you all things and will remind you of everything I have said to you. Peace I leave with you; my peace I give you. I do not give to you as the world gives. Do not let your hearts be troubled and do not be afraid."* (John 14:26–27)

A few years later, he writes this: "No one has ever seen God; but if we love one another, God lives in us and his love is made complete in us" (1 John 4:12).

We have the Spirit within us, we have God's people around us. When we cannot see, we are still seen.

That's why we can sing of our doubt, and watch it actually strengthen our faith.

It's like a muscle. The resistance in your exercise is what helps you grow. If you want to have stronger arms, you have to lift things that make your arms feel weak. The more you do that, the more your arms can lift.

By acknowledging and even singing about our doubt, we make room for the Spirit to begin to chip away at its power.

Don't think, though, that I'm painting you some rosy picture.

Doubting God is the loneliest place I've known. It has made me question everything about who I am and what I am and my place in my family, my community, and my own mind.

Do you know this feeling? When you're so deep in the valley that it's hard to even remember the mountaintop experience you used to think was your faith?

It's why I find such solace in these old songs. Knowing that others have been to this place too. I wish we had more songs like them today. We need them.

My friend Kevin, the one who taught us all about the great hymns, was particularly fond of the writer Anne Steele.

Her songs ache with beauty and carry a poetic passion uncommon in hymns of similar theological depth. She suffered greatly from her own illness and loneliness and multiple family deaths, and yet you can see in her writing the comfort and delight she found in Christ. The beautiful way she intertwines her doubts, suffering, and humanity with the beauty and glory of Jesus is astounding.

On the subject of doubt, in particular, here is one of my favorites of her verses:

> But oh! when gloomy doubts prevail,
> I fear to call thee mine;
> The springs of comfort seem to fail,
> And all my hopes decline.
> Yet gracious God, where shall I flee?
> Thou art my only trust,
> And still my soul would cleave to thee,
> Tho' prostrate in the dust.
>
> —"DEAR REFUGE OF MY WEARY SOUL," ANNE STEELE (1717–1778)

By singing honestly about our doubts, God can often mysteriously lead us to a deeper belief.

7.

Time

> O God, our Help in ages past,
> our Hope for years to come,
> be Thou our Guard while life shall last,
> and our eternal Home!
>
> —"O GOD, OUR HELP IN AGES PAST," ISAAC WATTS, 1719

TIME IS A SLIPPERY THING, isn't it? You know what it is until you try to define it, and then, suddenly, words start to fail you.

I wrote a song that talked about it years ago. "These days, they are a river, that we're all floating down."[1] There is no stopping that river, and we're all in the boat.

That's what I saw all throughout those old hymnals. The tenses: *The past, present, and future.*

Much of my career has been spent working directly with the creation and curation of worship music, and I will tell you that, whether you notice or not, almost all modern worship songs focus on the present.

We sing a lot about how God makes us feel, and what we are asking from God at this very moment. Our songs are intimate, personal, and very much in the *present* tense of experiencing the holy *presence* of God.

Each generation, and movement within it, can be summed up with a primary theme and, taken together over two thousand years, all of them might just start to hint at a complete picture of what it means to worship God. No one of them tells the full story. It's far too vast. We are a culture in touch with our feelings and it's natural that our worship of Him would follow that form.

When this era of sacred songs is studied a hundred years from now, I think they will say that its dominant subject was our emotional response to Immanuel's presence with us. This is our generation's offering and it's a beautiful one.

Yet, on this side of heaven, there's a pros and cons list to just about everything, it seems, and in this case focusing on the present has meant that we don't sing that much about what went before or what's coming up ahead, nor do we really ponder the mystery of a God who somehow mysteriously lives outside of time.

"You who live in eternity, hear the prayers of those of us who live in time," sang Rich Mullins, one of my songwriting heroes.[2]

As Christians, our past and our future are big deals. They define who we are.

From the very beginning, we have sung our past. The Psalms at times read like history lessons, full of names, places, and events. These were community songs used to shape and teach via oral tradition.

Songs are a great way to teach kids information. I bet it's still sort of how you know the alphabet. These psalms were probably a big part of how the actual *children* of the children of Israel learned their own history, that continual story of God's people breaking their promise, getting themselves into trouble, and God coming to rescue them.

"Amazing Grace," which is the Coldplay of hymns in that it's so popular you're surprised to remember it's also actually very good, is a late 1700s version of this kind of song.

Amazing grace, (how sweet the sound),
that saved a wretch like me,
I once was lost, but now am found,
was blind, but now I see.
—"AMAZING GRACE," JOHN NEWTON, 1779

Almost that whole first verse is about remembering what God did in the past, and where it has brought us. You see, those psalms aren't just about Israel being who they used to be, but who they are now because of what they'd gone through. They were delivered. Rescued.

We sing "Amazing Grace" because we've been rescued too.

We need to keep singing these songs because we, the rescued people, are also we, the forgetful people.

The Israelites grumbled in the desert, "Even slavery was better than this; let's go back!" How quickly they had forgotten the never-ending, soul-crushing, back-breaking oppression they had begged to be freed from.

Am I any different when it comes to my sin? With my wandering eye and envious heart? When my vision can get so clouded with anger that I can't even see to walk straight?

A story in the Bible tells about God helping Samuel win an unexpected triumph against a much more powerful enemy army. To remember how God saved and delivered them, he sets up an Ebenezer, or "a stone of help," as a memorial to God's faithfulness. "Thus far the LORD has helped us" (1 Sam. 7:12).

Back in 1758, Robert Robinson wrote a hymn and he actually used that word in the second verse: Ebenezer. Maybe people knew what it meant back then, but I grew up singing it and all I thought of was Donald Duck in *Mickey's Christmas Carol*. It wasn't until Kevin explained it to me when I was in my early twenties that I even understood what I was singing. Once you know the resonance of that word, though, and do a little unpacking of the old language, you get absolutely sucker-punched by the power of these words.

> *Here I raise my Ebenezer;*
> *hither by thy help I'm come;*
> *and I hope, by thy good pleasure,*
> *safely to arrive at home.*
> *Jesus sought me when a stranger,*
> *wandering from the fold of God;*
> *he, to rescue me from danger,*
> *interposed his precious blood.*
>
> —"COME, THOU FOUNT OF EVERY BLESSING," ROBERT ROBINSON, 1758

"Jesus sought me when a stranger, wandering from the fold of God." You could warm up the tattoo gun for that one. That's the past we need to remember and be reminded of, often, so that we can believe that He is actively working on our behalf now. This is where we find the hope for our future, after all.

That's right! Our future! Let's not forget about that! What a powerful and important thing to sing about. To remind ourselves of the great hope that we have ahead of us.

And yet again, forget we do. Go to most any evangelical church today, listen to the four or five current songs they're leading, and you very likely will hear little to no mention of the hope of the life to come. It is all about the right here, right now.

Songs of future tense are all throughout both the Bible and the old hymnbooks, across denominations. Back in 1873, the lesser-known last verse of Horatio Spafford's heartbreakingly magnificent hymn "It Is Well" goes like this:

> *O Lord, haste the day when my faith shall be sight,*
> *the clouds be rolled back as a scroll;*

the trump shall resound and the Lord shall descend;
even so, it is well with my soul.
—"IT IS WELL WITH MY SOUL," HORATIO SPAFFORD, 1873

What a powerful statement. What is it that keeps us shying away from songs like this today? (Again, I realize these are broad statements, and there are many wonderful exceptions.)

Well, perhaps we're just a little too comfortable. As I've said before, we keep our suffering and doubt hidden, even from ourselves, and so maybe we don't acutely feel the need that Christians in other times and places have felt. We're able to distract and insulate ourselves from the grief and pain that drove generations before us to look toward the hope of the life to come.

This is why it is vital that we sing of the past to remember God's faithfulness to us and sing of the future to remember that our hope is an eternity with Him. This gives us a different perspective on both the joys and the trials we experience here today.

Here's a lyric from a song almost a thousand years old, written in 1145 by Bernard of Clairvaux, a French priest:

Brief life is here our portion;
Brief sorrow, short-lived care:
The life that knows no ending,
The tearless life is there.

When our gaze is on today, our focus inevitably turns toward our circumstances and our feelings, and naturally, we do need to pay attention there. Hope, though, is what lets us lift our eyes and turn our gaze beyond—out to the horizon—past where we are, and onward to where we are going.

The hope of the new heavens and the new earth. The tearless "life that knows no ending" with Jesus.

Sounds like a pretty great time.

8.

Place

There is a place of quiet rest,
near to the heart of God.
—"NEAR TO THE HEART OF GOD," CLELAND BOYD MCAFEE, 1901

I WALK JUST ABOUT EVERY morning at a beautiful state park near my house called Radnor Lake.

The lake itself was made in 1913 as a reservoir to hold the water that would cool steam engines coming off the new railroad from Decatur, Alabama.

Here's a wild fact: All large lakes in Tennessee are man-made, except for Reelfoot Lake near Memphis, which was created during the winter of 1811–1812 when a series of earthquakes caused the Mississippi River to flow *backward*, and the water spilled over the banks, leaving a lake as a souvenir.

I have no idea why I know this tidbit.

I used to try and run in the mornings, but as I was leaving my last job and dealing with my wife's health (in September of 2023, Alison was diagnosed with a rare and aggressive blood cancer called multiple myeloma), I just felt like the rest of my life was "run, run, run" and I had negative gas in the tank for that. It was feeling vitally important, however, to be outside, to have some time alone, and to move my body.

Some people talk freely like "I felt God was saying to do this" or "God spoke to me about that," but personally, I've rarely had that kind of certain affirmation.

Maybe twice.

And I've spent years chasing it, sometimes faking it, trying to have it again.

If I ever write another book, maybe I'll unpack that. Who knows.

Anyway, I didn't hear a voice, but I did have an urge. A strong and spiritual feeling. A sacred longing, really, to just start walking outside. So I began every morning after I dropped my girls off at school, detouring over by the lake, taking a deep breath, and heading off into the woods.

I walk here on days when it's gorgeous, I walk here in the rain, in the summers when it's boiling, and the winter when it's stupid cold. I now try to take most of my business meetings here, if people are willing to meet me in a parking lot with no cell reception, and we walk around the lake for an hour.

I've been coming here long enough to watch fall roll into winter, and then I've seen the actual day that the green of spring started to pop out from nowhere. Every year it happens when I just about can't take the winter any longer. Will the winter ever end? A part of my soul starts to feel as barren as the trees, but then, suddenly, there it is. New life. Right on cue. My eyes get wet every time.

Spring turns to summer, and summer turns into a Tennessee autumn, which is the most magnificent thing you can even imagine. The hills are on fire. It takes your breath away and you wish it could last forever, but the days, they are a river . . .

This place is a promise.

My life has been full of winters. Yours probably has too. God has been faithful to this place before I've been coming here, and

He will stay faithful after I'm gone. It's His place, after all.

For a little bit, though, like a house or an apartment, this place gets to be my place too. It's where I get to welcome my friends, and I get to know the bends in the trails and hold memories of where I had this conversation or that moment of prayer.

My family knows that I'll have little to offer in a will, but that I hope they can put my name on one of the benches on the west side trails, so I can keep welcoming people here as long as possible.

Before God created humankind, He created the earth. A place. With its rhythms and its laws and its grandeur and its delicacy. And He called it good.

Jesus could have stayed in the ether, but He came to earth, to this place, to be with us. I love that the story of His life is so full of detail. He invested Himself in location. He was born in a barn in Bethlehem. He had to flee and become a refugee in Egypt, before being raised as a carpenter in Nazareth, a small town in the region of Galilee.

As Jesus finally stepped out of the shadows and onto the stage to begin His ministry, He gets baptized in the river Jordan and then immediately goes out to the desert. He leaves and goes out to the hills or the mountains all the time to pray. Maybe that's part of what called me out to the lake.

There was a song the old people would call out at every one of those Sunday night hymn sings when I was a kid:

> *I come to the garden alone,*
> *While the dew is still on the roses;*
> *And the voice I hear, falling on my ear,*
> *The Son of God discloses.*
> *And He walks with me, and He talks with me,*
> *And He tells me I am His own.*
>
> —"IN THE GARDEN," C. AUSTIN MILES, 1912

When my friend Rob first moved to Nashville, he didn't know many people here. He saw on social media that a number of folks he knew about seemed to frequent the same coffee shop. He was working remotely, so he decided to just bring his laptop to that coffee shop and work there all day, every day, until he could meet those people and become friends with them.

He did. That's how we became friends. He came to one of my places.

About a decade before I started walking around Radnor daily, there was one other season I went there often.

I've only had two "real" jobs in my life, and the first one did not end the way I'd hoped. All of a sudden, I was thirty-five with a wife, three kids, a mortgage, and no idea how to support them. The well-known Psalm 23 (ESV) says, "He leads me beside still waters" and since nothing in my life felt "still," I would go to the lake, the nearest water to my house, and walk around praying, sometimes out loud (sometimes very loud), "Okay, God, I'm here, where are You?"

Like Rob at the coffee shop, sometimes you have to go to the place, and wait.

Waiting for God to appear . . . isn't that something my kids do every December with a special calendar in the kitchen? Really, aren't our whole lives just Advent, waiting for the Messiah to return?

And yet, every December, while we're waiting, we flip to a different part of the songbook at Christmastime. We find ourselves singing the word "Immanuel," which means "God with us."

Even while we long for His presence and wait in our angst and our sorrow to hear His voice, He is the God who is *with* us. Always mysteriously and intimately with us, right where we are. We can go to the still waters to find Him, but it's not necessary.

He's already come to our places, wherever they are (and which were really His places in the first place).

9.

Faithfulness

Morning by morning new mercies I see.
All I have needed thy hand hast provided;
Great is thy faithfulness, Lord unto me.
—"GREAT IS THY FAITHFULNESS," THOMAS O. CHISHOLM, 1923

YEARS AGO, I LOST A job and spent a few months spiraling into a bit of a depression. I had to support three kids, a wife, and a mortgage and had no clue how I was going to pull it all off. One evening I was in the kitchen, trying to hide my inner panic from my family, when my wife, Alison, found one of the girls' teachers on Instagram.

"Look, girls! It's Miss what's-her-name," and she held the phone up for us to see. There under her name the teacher had a little quote: "Morning by morning, new mercies I see."

You might recognize that line. It's a lyric from one of the most popular hymns of the past century, "Great Is Thy Faithfulness," which also happens to be one of my personal favorites. I know it by heart, and the melody immediately started playing in my mind, so the next line then rang out into my heart: "All I have needed, thy hand has provided; Great is thy faithfulness, Lord, unto me."

Something about that lyric in that moment was like a tranquilizer dart to me. As worried as I had been, I was suddenly flooded with a peace I could not explain. My problems were bigger than I could handle myself, and I knew that. Someone else had to help me. It would take someone more powerful, with more resources and more wisdom, to help my marriage, my girls, my empty bank account, and my reputation . . .

I don't think I had the ability to put it into words then, but if I had, it might have been: "Lord, Your faithfulness to me is great, even greater than my problems, which feel pretty gigantic at the moment."

That quiet, unexplainable peace stayed with me for weeks. It was a holy gift, giving me space to finally catch my breath and rest, and eventually even find a path out of that season's valley.

I'm not a guy who has had a lot of supernatural experiences, so I've never really told anyone about it until, well, right now, actually. It didn't seem like a big deal. Just a sweet relief. But that first night, I slept like a baby, something I hadn't done in months. The next morning, I woke up with a business idea (a podcast) that a year later ended up having turned my career around. (One by-product, incidentally, is this very book you're currently reading.)

Something changed for me that day. Not the circumstances of my situation. Not immediately. That took a while. But my inner posture. And it was not my doing. God did something in me.

In my life, though, He almost never shows up to me like He did that one night (or year, depending on how you look at it). That was a unique time I could clearly define what His faithfulness looked like. More often, it has not been as glaringly obvious, at least not in the moment.

If you feel like God's work in your life is often subtle, or something you understand better in retrospect, then take heart. If you can see how He has cared for you at some point in your past, that means in the future you might one day also look back and see the hand of God in ways you could not imagine.

God's love for us is so much bigger and wilder than we can comprehend that it extends beyond the spectrum of colors our human eyes can see. That our hearts can't recognize what He's doing in the moment is not surprising, though it can leave us stumbling in the darkness when we're surrounded by the light.

Thankfully, we have these melodies calling to us through the mist, anchoring us to the truths of our faith.

"Great Is Thy Faithfulness." I've sung this hymn literally hundreds of times, and on pretty much zero other occasions has it brought about any sort of miracle or super spiritual experience, but I still love singing it.

As a musician, I'm in awe of its construction. It's a stunning melody, with some quite adventurous chords. Every time record companies tell me that churches need songs to be overly simple so people can sing along, I point them to this song, which is anything but. It's complex, evocative, and utterly beautiful.

(Also, if an arena can sing along to every note of all five key changes of Beyonce's "Love on Top," church folks can handle a major 2 chord every now and then.)

The power of its lyrics, though, is just as, if not more, compelling. In my suffering, in my doubt, in every time, in every place, there is never a moment I am not in some form of need. I am always—*always*—at the mercy of God's faithfulness.

Thomas Chisholm, who wrote the lyrics to "Great Is Thy Faithfulness," wrote hundreds of hymns and sacred poems over his lifetime.[3] "Having been led, for a part of my life," he once said, "through some difficult paths, I have sought to gather from such experiences, material out of which to write hymns of comfort and cheer for those similarly circumstanced." He said that "his aim was to incorporate as much of Scripture as possible and to avoid flippant or sentimental themes."[4]

Isn't sentimentality—an exaggeration or excessive expression of emotion—the very opposite of faithfulness, in a way? At its core, we know that sweetness for the sake of sweetness is hollow. We can tell when someone says they care but doesn't mean it. We know what it feels like when someone tearfully tells you at the end of summer camp that they'll always be your friend, but when you call them a month later, they've forgotten about you.

Sentimentality hurts so deeply because it's a lie about something we desperately want to believe. *I want you to love me, you say that you do, but I know that you don't mean it.* That's devastating. Two levels of brutality. *You don't love me and you're lying to me.*

At its core, I believe this is why some of today's modern worship songs can cause unintentional harm.

If there's something about these songs that doesn't ring quite true, either because of poor theology, an attempt at marketability, or just plain bad writing (or a combination of the three), we feel it. This might look like pulling Scripture out of context, choosing "positivity" over honesty, or just making something sacred feel trivial.

When we sing together in worship, we are singing about God and love and hope and truth, all things we so desperately need and care about. If they ring hollow, it stings. These aren't pop songs that we assume to be shallow; we need these songs to mean something.

At their worst, they are offering sentimentality when we have an urgent thirst to hear and sing (and taste and drink) of the deep well of God's faithfulness.

We know that when we're grieving or freaking out or in really great need, we do not want a sentimental, smiling Jesus—we need the Man of Sorrows, well acquainted with grief. The one who sat with sinners and blessed His enemies.

Mercifully, our God is not sentimental.

He is faithful.

In our suffering, God is not telling us to cheer up and get over it or smile and act like everything is okay. He is there with us: "The Lord is close to the brokenhearted and saves those who are crushed in spirit" (Ps. 34:18). "He will take great delight in you; in his love he will no longer rebuke you, but will rejoice over you with singing" (Zeph. 3:17). And He is faithful.

In our doubt, He is not giving us cheesy slogans or moral platitudes. He is there and He is faithful.

In our past, our present, and our future, He was with us, He is with us now, and He will be forever. He is faithful.

Wherever we may be. If we fall in love and win the lottery, if our nation is at war and we've lost everything, He is with us and He is faithful.

If we rise on the wings of the dawn, if we make our bed in the depths, if we settle on the far side of the sea, even still . . .

All that we need His hands will provide. Great is His faithfulness to us.

10.

Joy

Love divine, all loves excelling,
joy of Heav'n to Earth come down.
—"LOVE DIVINE, ALL LOVES EXCELLING," CHARLES WESLEY, 1747

JOY IS A SHORT WORD that holds many meanings. It can mean happiness, like the feeling I get when I hear my children's laughter, see the shimmer on Radnor Lake, or get swept away in a beautiful melody—though I prefer to think of these more as fruit on the sturdy branches of joy's tree.

Joy is steadfast; it's able to stand firm in stormy weather, because its roots are seasoned and deep. Ultimately, those roots must go deeper than ourselves, as we know that we ourselves are unrooted people.

Joy does not advertise. Rather, it is a disposition, a way of thinking and living and seeing the world. It's a lightness and a kindness that comes from being aware that you are not in control—and knowing and trusting the One who is.

Stories about joy in the Bible are resplendent.

We have Paul and Silas, singing in the jail cell. Sarah and Abraham, finally finding joy upon Isaac's birth after many disappointing years. We see the pictures of the early church, filled with joy and praising God together even through challenging times, sharing everything they had in community. Ultimately, we have Jesus' parables about what was lost being found: a sheep, a coin, a son.

In each of these stories, the joy comes after, or in the midst of, some sort of suffering.

Ah, yes. There's that word again. Against all instinct, wisdom teaches us that suffering is the doorway to joy.

> *I've found a joy in sorrow,*
> *A secret balm for pain,*
> *A beautiful tomorrow*
> *Of sunshine after rain.*
> —"I'VE FOUND A JOY IN SORROW" JANE FOX CREWDSON (1840–1908)

It's not that pain, by itself, is the key; rather, it places choices before us that may lead us down a path we could not find any other way.

Among these choices are:

What will we do with our anger?
Will we be honest with God about what is broken about our world and ourselves?
What will we do with our desires?
Dare we bring to God our deepest longings and trust that He cares?
Can we let go of our need to be right? To be the hero?
Can we lay down our weapons?
Can we be grateful?

Here we see that Christ has gone before us. The Man of Sorrows quotes this psalm as His final words before He dies: "Into your hands I commit my spirit" (Luke 23:46, quoting Ps. 31:5).

He lays His life down. He surrenders. And in His giving up everything, the whole course of history is changed.

Joy

The course of my own life was changed by suffering, surrender, and joy as well. I remember one moment so clearly.

I was sitting at a coffee shop with my friend Russ, exhausted and numb.

My wife, Alison, and I had just had our third baby and had spent the past month at a YoungLife camp, where I was volunteering as the music leader. I had invested nearly every dime we had into an album that would release that fall, when I would go on tour to earn back the investment.

Two days before our return I had gotten a phone call from a neighbor. Something was wrong at our house. A water pipe in our hall bathroom had burst and had been running for weeks, flooding the entire house. Water had filled up the space above the basement ceiling and below the main floor of our little 1960s ranch, until the whole thing collapsed.

We lost almost everything.

They took the house down to the studs. We had to live in an apartment with rented silverware and borrowed toys. The place had barely any windows, and the constant darkness only added to our stress. The bank that stood between us and our insurance company would later receive the largest fine in US history for fraud and we were in line to become one of its victims.

Alison is a strong, resilient, and vibrantly playful soul, but this season was a brutal one—cooped up in those four sad walls with two young girls, a newborn, a never-ending stream of discouraging obstacles, and a frustrated husband making a series of stupid and impulsive decisions.

I've probably had four years like that now, where every day just seems harder than the last, and you think, "How long can this go on?" (Of course, many of the psalmists asked God that very question too. How oddly comforting that is.)

Somewhere in the foggy mist of those days, Russ and I met at that coffee shop. I don't even drink coffee. We sat down and just silently looked at each other. Finally, he handed me a folded-up piece of paper. On it was a black and white printed-out picture of a kitten hanging from a tree that said, "Hang In There."

From deep inside me, uncontrollably, I just burst out laughing. Russ did too. We awkwardly, embarrassingly, publicly, cry-laughed for probably two or three minutes, which is a lot longer in real life than it is to read about. It was so dumb—and exactly what I needed. I was so grateful.

In this season, the world had handed me some of the hardest things I'd ever faced, and some of the stupid ways I'd tried to handle the pressure of it all ended up causing even more damage than the initial problems themselves. The weight was crushing, and then the shame was overwhelming.

Yet it was also in this season that a sort of springtime began to appear. It was so clear to me that fixing this mess was beyond my power. Once I realized that, I surprisingly found myself in a sort of freedom. If we were going to get through this, it'd be only due to God. There was simply no way I could do it.

Instead, my sheer powerlessness was offering me a choice: bitterness or gratitude.

After years of leaning into bitterness, in this darkest season I now felt God pulling me toward gratitude. I started being more thankful for the friends and family I had taken for granted. For the stuff we had saved from the flood. For the cat that said, "Hang In There."

Choosing gratitude, even in my suffering, has been the most beautiful surrender, and the full bloom of that gratitude has been joy.

I have tasted the fruit of that tree, more and more as the years go on, and it is real and good. Even as storms hit hard—and oh, friends, are they vicious—the roots are deep and the soil is eternal.

It didn't happen quickly; the best things rarely do. But little by little, joy was coming to my world.

I love that every December we get to hear songs that echo that same story, in and out of the church, everywhere we go.

> *Melt the clouds of sin and sadness;*
> *Drive the dark of doubt away*
> —"JOYFUL, JOYFUL, WE ADORE THEE," HENRY VAN DYKE, 1907

> *No more let sins and sorrows grow,*
> *Nor thorns infest the ground;*
> *He comes to make his blessings flow*
> *Far as the curse is found.*
>
> *Joy to the world; the Lord is come!*
> —"JOY TO THE WORLD," ISAAC WATTS, 1719

> *Shepherds, why this jubilee?*
> *Why your joyous strains prolong?*
> *What the gladsome tidings be*
> *which inspire your heav'nly song?*
> *Gloria in excelsis Deo!*
> —"ANGELS WE HAVE HEARD ON HIGH," TRADITIONAL FRENCH CAROL

Why were the shepherds so glad? Why will sin, sadness, and doubt be driven away?

Joy was coming to earth, the land of shadows and curses and sorrow, in the form of God Himself.

11.

Peace

> *O God of love, O King of peace,*
> *Make wars throughout the world to cease;*
> *Our greed and violent ways restrain.*
> *Give peace, O God, give peace again.*
> —"O GOD OF LOVE, O KING OF PEACE," H. W. BAKER, 1861

PEACE, WE MUST UNDERSTAND, IS more than a cozy afternoon or a quiet walk in a park, though it certainly includes those things. When the "park" lies under the rubble of years of mortar blasts, as it does for so many of our brothers and sisters around the world, we must realize the word holds a much deeper power.

We'll see how long it lasts, but the United States has mostly gone since the 1860s without a war on our soil, and thus we might take the word "peace" for granted.

If there's been a war within your family or your living room, though, you most certainly do not.

We are created for a union with God that is not fully possible in our broken human world, and because we cannot perfectly fill this longing, that absence is the fuel that drives us to chase relationships or success or escape or popularity or whatever it is that burns within us. Ultimately, we are desperate to feel that we are known and loved by God, and when we don't feel that, hell breaks loose. The world is not at peace.

When we cry out to God, we are crying out for peace, to make the striving and fighting and even the longing stop and let us rest in His presence.

Because peace implies calm, we can be fooled into thinking it is a passive thing, but what a mistake this would be.

Peace, we must recognize, is a constant, conscious, willful activity that requires care, maintenance, and continued investment.

What we often think of as peace is actually the result of its labor: rest, stillness, relaxation, an end to the fighting, the laying down of swords, the rebuilding of what has been destroyed, and so on.

There's a great Charles Wesley line in his classic Christmas hymn "Hark! The Herald Angels Sing" where he calls Jesus "the heaven-born Prince of Peace." What a brilliant thought. The Son of the King of peace, born in heaven, which He left to make peace here on earth.

Before this reconciliation, however, there was a greater peace, before suffering and beyond time, hovering above the waters.

This "blessed Trinity"—Father, Son, and Holy Spirit—existed in perfect unity, a dance of eternal friendship, until the deliberate and conscious decision for Jesus to, as Wesley beautifully phrased it in "And Can It Be," leave "his Father's throne above."

Peace is not passive. Peace is action, and peace has a price tag.

And so it is that peace for the Christian rests on this brutal and beautiful truth: "God demonstrates his own love for us in this: While we were still sinners, Christ died for us" (Rom. 5:8).

God has made peace for us.

If you actually look closely, we don't sing about this as much as you might think we do these days. We bristle at some of the language, partly because some of those words don't market-test very well and partly because maybe we really are a bit uncomfortable ourselves with the word "sin" and what it says about us and the things we like to do.[5]

Yet, this is the heart of what is so precious about the gospel of Jesus Christ. It holds the key to the peace we're all so desperately hungry for.

> *Peace, perfect peace, in this dark world of sin?*
> *The blood of Jesus whispers peace within.*
> —"PEACE, PERFECT PEACE," EDWARD HENRY BICKERSTETH JR., 1875

> *This is all my hope and peace:*
> *nothing but the blood of Jesus.*
> *This is all my righteousness:*
> *nothing but the blood of Jesus.*
> —"NOTHING BUT THE BLOOD OF JESUS," ROBERT LOWRY, 1876

Because Christ has made this peace with the consequence of sin and death, He is able to be a safe haven. A shelter. A harbor. There is peace. The war is over. Those who once were enemies are now friends, even family.

We need these songs of comfort and safety and, thankfully, our church today has a wealth of them. Sunday mornings in America vibrate with melodies of God's love and nurture; with how much He knows us and cares for us. In a cynical culture that so often views human life as not much more than the sum of our clicks and our portfolios, we can never hear too much about the love and peace of God.

Ultimately, though, the peace that God gives us is not simply for us alone, and this is where our songs do fall sadly short today. "Love one another. As I have loved you, so you must love one another" was Christ's commandment in John 13:34. We are charged to "pass the peace" that God has given us and make peace with and for others.

> *In Christ now meet both east and west,*
> *in him meet south and north.*
> *All Christly souls are joined as one*
> *throughout the whole wide earth.*
>
> —"IN CHRIST THERE IS NO EAST OR WEST,"
> JOHN OXENHAM (PSEUDONYM FOR WILLIAM ARTHUR DUNKERLEY), 1908

Francis of Assisi (1181–1126), the well-known Italian friar, gave us these timeless words:

> *Make me a channel of your peace:*
> *Where there is hatred, let me bring your love;*
> *where there is injury, your healing power,*
> *and where there's doubt, true faith in you.*

My heart aches almost every time I see the word "Christian" used in the news these days, whatever the political bent of the source, for the name is too often attached to scandal, cruelty, and corruption. Rarely, if ever, do we see the posture of peace and humility of these hymns shining through.

I realize that the good, slow work of the fruit of the Spirit and the making of peace does not generate the same social media clicks as outrage and scandal, but that knowledge doesn't lessen the sting.

I grew up singing "They'll know we are Christians by our love," and I believe that to the core of my being.

"Dona Nobis Pacem" is a traditional Latin hymn that means "Grant us peace." Often, it is sung as a round, with voices adding in as the song grows, together in harmony, as a group of Christians collectively, meditatively, ask God for this action of peace in their lives and community. If you're not familiar with it, it's well worth finding on YouTube.

What would it look like for us to do this today? To add our voices and let a song of active, conscious, willful peace grow—sung and practiced by brothers and sisters laying down their swords and rebuilding together what the world has destroyed?

What if the world knew we were Christians by our love, and by the peace that we worked for and nurtured?

God has made peace with us and for us, and in response, we are charged to make peace with others and for others.

Dona Nobis Pacem.

12.

I Need to Hear You

A DIGRESSION

WHAT A STRANGE AND INTIMATE gift it is to stand next to someone and hear them sing.

To think how we in the church do this so regularly that we take it for granted is wild. In no other context would sober people who aren't in a choir or a class do such a thing. Yet, week after week, we do.

There we are, beside a friend, a spouse, a parent, a teacher, a fellow member of our local community and, assuming the music leading us is not so loud to drown it out, we get to hear their voices . . .

. . . confessing their need and reminding us that we are not alone in our sin and limitations.

. . . affirming their belief and encouraging us that we are not crazy to put our hope in Jesus. (Or if we are, at least we're not the only ones!)

. . . praising the God we long so desperately to connect with, to be healed by, and to thank for all that we hold so dear.

When we feel the cruelty of the world, we hear the voices—actually, we *are* the voices—of God's children, crying together for justice.

In the dark of winter, we hear each other join with the angels, "Joy to the world, the Lord is come!"

When we witness the waking of spring, we hear our friends cry out "He is risen!"

The voices we hear celebrating at our wedding feasts are the same that mourn by our gravesides.

When God's people first started meeting together, they could have been organized to sit and listen to the most talented voices, but God knew that is not what we needed, so He asked that we sing together. To plead and praise together. And a beautiful, and surely intentional, by-product is that we get to hear one another doing so. Because we need it.

I need to hear you, and you need to hear me.

Yet, there is so much at work to keep this gift of connectedness from us, whether it be our society's introduction of lights and sound systems and the blurred lines of worship leading and performance, or our own personal shame and insecurities. And trust me, I understand shame and insecurity, but here's something I've learned the hard way:

Friends, please don't believe the lie that the quality of your voice equates to its value. Evil would love nothing more.

Know that every voice is a blessing to someone.

To my regret, my ears were not always attuned to these more "sacred frequencies."

In years past, when I would be standing in worship singing, or leading from the stage, and I'd hear a loud, sometimes awkward, or distracting voice, my first instinct was to be annoyed and question why they weren't "reading the room" like everyone else. Or even worse, I would look around, in hopes of locking eyes with a friend, so we could share a laugh at the expense of this "pioneering vocalist."

Lord, have mercy.

Of course, after the show I'd meet a family who was sitting in that section of the room and find out that a giant fan of mine has special needs and loved to sing along at the top of his lungs to every song. (*Yeah, Andrew, this is what you thought was so funny.*)

If Christ's kindness is found in our continual humbling, then Jesus has been exceptionally kind to me. Yet, I'm thankful, even for the many times I've made a fool of myself, for God has used it as a great teacher.

And so, I've been led to this understanding, that every Sunday, as I'm there in a room full of people who know me and my family, as we know and love theirs, that I am surrounded by what Martin Luther called "the priesthood of all believers": the Holy Spirit alive and faithful in the hearts all around me.

I promise you, that is infinitely more powerful than a great video package and even the most inspiring worship leader.

As I get older, I am bringing more and more into church with me (our children's relationships, my wife's cancer, my career, our finances, national politics, and so on). It now matters less and less to me how great the worship team sounds, and so much more that I hear the hope and belief in the voices of people I love singing along around me.

THE MYSTERIES

We can find almost as many types of songs as there are people on the planet, and anytime there's an attempt to divide them into a category of "all this" versus "all that," we inevitably end up seeing all the many outliers and exceptions.

And yet, when it comes to the sacred songs we sing together, patterns do emerge.

We might sing in the first person, the third, or even the second—meaning we might sing to God, about God, or even occasionally from the perspective of God Himself. However, while fascinating, that's not the distinction that surprised me on my journey into the old hymnals.

There was a fascinating boundary line that stood out to me in the Sunday morning songs of our past. We sang, and still sing, hymns primarily about us and how God meets us.

Then we turned our gaze and sang about God and what we know of Him, which is by its nature a little harder to grasp and more mysterious. We still do this too.

We've talked about the *us-focused* themes of our suffering and doubt, in time and place, and God's faithfulness to us through all those, leading us to joy and peace.

Now let's explore what the other sacred songs have to tell us *about God Himself*. His presence, His glory, His goodness, and His otherness.

Follow me, won't you, into the mysteries . . .

13.

Presence

O wide-embracing, wondrous love,
We read Thee in the sky above;
We read Thee in the earth below,
In seas that swell and streams that flow.
—"O LOVE OF GOD, HOW STRONG AND TRUE," HORATIUS BONAR, 1861

I DON'T DRINK COFFEE.

It's a strange habit to not have for a guitar player/record label guy who hangs out in recording studios and writes books in his spare time. The only real disadvantage, though, is that coffee drives you to coffee shops where you would be more likely to run into people, sit across from them, and get to know them, and I wish I had more of that in my life.

As a guy who would fail a personality test on the line between introvert and extrovert, I'm always grateful for built-in ways of getting to know people.

It's only been the last few years, however, that I've realized that sitting across from people is not always the best way to make friends. Most of my closest and longest friendships were not developed across from each other, but rather side by side: working on a project, standing on the sidelines as our kids played soccer, and yes, of course, walking around the lake.

In fact, many friendships weren't even built with that level of intention. We were just hanging around. We worked in the same office, or were in the same class or small group, or we just kind of ended up at the same stuff all the time.

"How do you guys know each other?"

"I don't know... we just sort of do."

I've spent enough time in Christian circles to become familiar with the idea that God pursues me. There are times, in some form or another, that I've felt that sacred and holy intention. Like He's invited me for coffee (or tea or whatever) and we've talked.

In my experience, it's more as though God has just kind of been everywhere that I end up going. It's like we're into the same bands and enjoy the same Thai places.

I say that like it's been clear or I understand it, but it usually hasn't and I generally don't. It's more often looked something like...

God's provision is not a shout; finding that gift card was a whisper.

His love was not a bear hug; the rain my new trees needed was a nod across the room.

His judgment was not a hammer; that laptop battery just died at a very helpful time.

But then, suddenly, sometimes He's so real that everything else around you starts to feel like it got thrown into Photoshop and the little transparency slider starts moving, fading everything else out so you can see through it by percentage, and He's the only thing that's fully real.

Words will fall short in explaining the feeling, because words can't. Just like I can't plan for this kind of experience or make it happen on my own.

Truthfully, I probably feel like that transparency slider myself. About 80 percent of me wants that kind of experience to happen all the time, and 20 percent of me is just fine without it ever again.

Because in some ways, it's terrifying. God is, in some ways, terrifying. I do not understand Him, and I am ultimately the most scared of what I cannot understand.

To think about my suffering or my joy is something I can *kind* of handle, even when I can't handle it, because at least I know what it is. But to think about God suddenly being there, with *His* transparency slider on full blast? It's overwhelming.

God is so present that it drowns out all other presence around Him.

Critics of modern worship music will sometimes pick on what we sing today by calling them "love songs to Jesus" or even "Jesus-is-my-boyfriend songs." While I can be critical as well, I've tried my best to let my criticism be constructive, and to use my roles in the industry to put my assessments to good use.

That being said, our focus on God's presence today is almost entirely intimate. "This is what God's presence feels like *to me*." While not a bad thing in the slightest, it is far from complete.

Genesis 1 opens with God's presence, *and there was not a human in sight*.

In Exodus 3:14, God said to Moses, "I AM WHO I AM."

If a tree falls in the forest, God hears it. He is present with or without a human there.

God's presence is not contingent on us.

The 1867 hymn "Immortal, Invisible" talks about God just like that. He is light, yet we cannot see Him. He is not resting, but also not hurried. He is eternal and unchanging, yet the source of all fleeting life that quickly blossoms, flourishes, withers, and perishes. He is—in a word—*present*.

> *Immortal, invisible, God only wise,*
> *in light inaccessible hid from our eyes,*
> *most blessed, most glorious, the Ancient of Days,*
> *almighty, victorious, thy great name we praise.*
> —"IMMORTAL, INVISIBLE, GOD ONLY WISE," WALTER C. SMITH, 1867

I love that hymn, and particularly the next phrase, from verse 2: "Unresting, unhasting, and silent as light." Silent as light? I hope somebody was in the room with composer Walter Smith when he wrote that line, because that man deserved a high five.

God's existence and grandeur would be worth singing about, whether or not He paid our debts or made us feel comforted. His sheer presence alone is magnificent.

"I am the Alpha and the Omega, the First and the Last, the Beginning and the End." (Rev. 22:13)

And yet, that vast, mysterious, un-understandable, unknowable, omni-Presence has made Himself known to us. So we can sing songs of His boundless being like the one above, and we can also sing of God's deep intimate companionship, like my all-time favorite hymn here, which includes these lyrics:

> *Can we find a friend so faithful*
> *who will all our sorrows share?*
> *Jesus knows our every weakness;*
> *take it to the Lord in prayer!*
>
> *Do your friends despise, forsake you?*
> *Take it to the Lord in prayer!*
> *In his arms he'll take and shield you;*
> *you will find a solace there.*
> —"WHAT A FRIEND WE HAVE IN JESUS," JOSEPH SCRIVEN, 1855

The immeasurable existence of "I am who I am" is ever and always by our side. Walking together or working side by side (or yes, even over coffee), God's expansive, incomprehensible presence is wondrously present here with us.

14.

Glory

I am here to love you, dear
I'm putting up the dishes and taking out the trash
I could have gone out with the boys
But I'm here for you, no need to ask

That's how everybody's going to know how much I love you
'Cause I'm going to tell everybody so loudly
Yeah, everybody's going to know that I love you
They'll know you're great 'cause I'm loving you so loudly
—"LOOK AT ME, LOOKING AT YOU," BY ME, RIGHT NOW

IF I WROTE THIS LOVE song for my wife and it became a giant hit, I'm fairly certain no amount of royalties could ever cover the counseling bills the song would also generate.

Clearly, the hero of the song is not the one being sung to. I get this feeling sometimes (maybe a lot of times) in how we sing about God's glory in our modern Sunday morning songs.

"I lift my hands to praise you," we say. "Let's make a holy noise" and "The whole earth is going to hear us praise!" Often, we follow by telling God all that we'll do for Him. "I surrender everything," we say. "I'm laying down my life and giving You everything."[6]

It sounds so good and it feels so holy and sometimes we mean it so much. We really, truly do.

Other times maybe we feel more like Cogsworth's response to Disney's Beast.

"What should I get her?"

"Well, there's the usual things. Flowers, chocolates, promises you don't intend to keep."

The Bible has a few core themes it comes back to again and again. One of them is that God and mankind both make promises, but only God ever keeps them.

While there is surely a place for us to respond, like David in Psalm 57: "I will praise you, Lord, among the nations; I will sing of you among the peoples. For great is your love, reaching to the heavens; your faithfulness reaches to the skies" (vv. 9–10), our songs can jump straight to that response, sometimes skipping over what we're praising God for and, if we're not careful, that can make us the hero of our own worship songs.

Listen for it next week. There are many wonderful exceptions, and I hope your experience proves me wrong, but I know the worship charts well enough to know that many people reading this will, this Sunday, be joining in song where the focus is on what *we are going to do*, rather than what *God has done*. We will sing of the promises we make, instead of the promises God has kept, and kept at great cost.

This is all to say: The church in America, my friends, has a glory problem.

We like it. Of course we do, and our screens and lights and stadium seating and sound systems and all the rest give us a little bitty baby feeling of glory every week as we walk into the room. It can give those of us standing up on stage a lot of it. (If there's not a headline in the news today about where that ends, sadly just wait a couple days and there will be one soon.)

Any glory we might actually have, however, is like that of the moon—simply the reflection of the sun back toward itself, mercifully sharing some beauty and guidance down toward others who might need it.

If we look to songs of generations past, we can find lyrics and melodies that soar to the heavens and crash to the seas in their attempt to echo and honor the glory and magnificence of our Creator King.

"To God be the glory, great things He has done!" wrote Fanny Crosby in 1875.

I love how eloquently she sets this up. What exactly did God do, Fanny?

> *So loved He the world that He gave us His Son,*
> *who yielded His life an atonement for sin,*
> *and opened the life-gate that all may go in.*

So, what do we do in response? She gives it to us in this rousing chorus.

> *Praise the Lord! Praise the Lord,*
> *Let the earth hear His voice!*
> *Praise the Lord! Praise the Lord!*
> *Let the people rejoice!*
> *O come to the Father through Jesus the Son*
> *And give Him the glory, great things He has done!*

There is no doubt in that song who the hero is.

> *All hail the power of Jesus' name!*
> *Let angels prostrate fall.*

> *Bring forth the royal diadem,*
> *and crown him Lord of all.*
>
> *Let every tongue and every tribe*
> *responsive to his call,*
> *to him all majesty ascribe,*
> *and crown him Lord of all.*
> —"ALL HAIL THE POWER OF JESUS' NAME," EDWARD PERRONET, 1780

It's likely a product of our greater "me-centered" society, but the focus of most of our culture's church songs is based around our own personal narrative. Our songs about God are really about how *we* feel about God. With the best of intentions, we have let words be put in our mouths and songs get stuck in our heads that subtly suggest to us that we're at the heart of the action, making the decisions and claiming the victories.

The reframing we need is beyond some idea that God is the Sheriff and we're His deputies. God is not just the best of the good guys in the story, He is the writer and the story itself.

15.

Righteousness and Justice

> *He comes to break oppression,*
> *to set the captive free;*
> *to take away transgression,*
> *and rule in equity.*
>
> —"HAIL TO THE LORD'S ANOINTED," JAMES MONTGOMERY, 1821

THEOPHILUS GOULD "T. G." STEWARD was a young AME (African Methodist Episcopal) minister shortly after the Civil War, active in Reconstruction politics in the American South. When he was twenty-five years old, the first church he pastored, in Macon, Georgia, was burned down in "a mysterious fire."

Though born into a family of free Blacks, T. G. Steward was still a Black man during the Jim Crow era and certainly knew much about injustice. Yet he pushed on and accomplished amazing things, receiving his Doctorate of Divinity from Wilberforce University in Ohio, where he eventually became a professor. He authored eight books and mastered four languages. His wife, Dr. Susan Smith McKinney, would become the third African-American physician in the country.

From the ages of 48 to 63 he was appointed chaplain for the 25th US Infantry, one of the racially segregated regiments also known as the Buffalo Soldiers. Upon leaving the army, Steward was a part of a group that founded and led the American Negro Academy, where a community of African American scholars, authors, and activists worked to study African American history and promote the ideas of civil rights and equality. He was active in this work until his death in 1924, at age eighty.

His journals and letters are kept in the archives of the New York Public Library. His portrait hangs in the Smithsonian.[7]

As incredible and noteworthy as it was, the life of T. G. Steward was marked from beginning to end by a cruel and inhuman racial injustice. That some of his dying work was arguing for the dignity and humanity of his own existence, let alone that of his family's and his community's, is a heartbreaking shame.

Steward was a prolific writer—books, sermons, letters, essays, and so on—yet in all of his work, as far as I can tell, there is but one song. A life so full, who traveled the world and achieved amazing things against such great adversity, and who witnessed firsthand the evils of war, slavery, and oppression ... what kind of song do you think that one song might be?

Beautifully, it's a hymn of worship called "We'll Praise the Lord." Each verse extols a different aspect of God to praise: *He is great, He is wise, He is just, He is true, He is love.*

I'm particularly interested in that third verse. What prompts a man who has spent a lifetime under injustice to choose this attribute, specifically, for us to sing about?

> *We'll praise the Lord for He is just,*
> *And in Him we may ever trust;*
> *Princes and kings may turn aside,*
> *But God by right will e'er abide.*

> *Oh, we will praise Him,*
> *Oh, we will praise Him,*
> *Oh, we will praise His holy name.*

Theophilus Steward longed for, and deserved, justice. Because he had studied the Bible, he knew that, in the end, only in God's judgment could justice be secured, and he knew that God alone was righteous and trustworthy.

A lot of words in that last paragraph show up, not just in Steward's song, but on virtually every page of every hymnal on my shelf.

Righteousness. Justice. Secure. Trust. Judgment.

One of these words may not turn up on the screens of your church this weekend. Which do you think it is?

These are all squeamish words, and to be fair, it's not all their fault. They get a bad rap from their out-of-town cousins. Self-righteousness is ugly. Social justice is polarizing. *(He's a good guy, but not very fun at parties.)* Insecurity made middle school miserable. Trust is actually all right; we just have a few issues . . . but judgment?

Judgment is the Ultimate Big Bad.

"How dare you judge me?" might be the emotional ethos of our generation. We are an individualized culture, and we have taken the idea of judgment to mean an affront to our personal choices.

But when I think about a young T. G. Steward's church burning in the night, I want judgment. When I see people driving by, yelling cruel things at our neighbor with special needs, I want judgment. The list could go on forever. You can make your own. We know the world is broken, which tells us there is some kind of standard that describes the unbroken in the first place. The standard of things being right.

Righteousness.

For God to be truly good to us, to be our protector and our defender, He must be just. He must be secure. He must be able to lay down judgment against evil, which He can only do because He Himself is...

Righteousness.

Here again, because we don't like words that make us feel uncomfortable, we tend to sing about the effects without the cause. Not talking about it or singing about it doesn't make it untrue, however; but tragically, it leaves us unaware of the power of its truth.

I need to know that God will judge wickedness. When my kid gets bullied on the playground, I might be big enough to stop it and make things okay, but most of the evil in the world is too big for me to do anything about. My stomach gets tied up in knots sometimes, churning with angst and fury over evil politicians, ruining people's lives so they can have more power, or giant corporations destroying square miles of forest to make a nickel, or polluting the water supply of a community they know does not have the social capital to stop them.

"Why won't anyone do something about it?!" I want to scream to the heavens.

I wouldn't be the first.

Psalm 10:1–2 says:

> *Why, LORD, do you stand far off?*
> *Why do you hide yourself in times of trouble?*
> *In his arrogance the wicked man hunts down the weak,*
> *who are caught in the schemes he devises.*

Most scholars believe this psalm was a continuation of Psalm 9, which begins with the heading "For the director of music." That means Psalm 10 was also likely meant to be sung.

Can you imagine your local church singing *"Why, Lord, do you stand far off?"* in between "Great Are You, Lord" and "In Christ Alone"?

Flip the pages a bit and you come to Psalm 76:6–9. Also meant to be sung in communal worship.

> *At your rebuke, God of Jacob,*
> *both horse and chariot lie still.*
> *It is you alone who are to be feared.*
> *Who can stand before you when you are angry?*
> *From heaven you pronounced judgment,*
> *and the land feared and was quiet—*
> *when you, God, rose up to judge,*
> *to save all the afflicted of the land.*

I won't lie, there are a lot of Sundays when I could imagine that these words hanging in the air over my family and friends would be just what I needed. It's a reminder that God hears us and will rescue us, making right what has gone so wrong.

That's why a song like this has such power:

> *Fear not, I am with thee, O be not dismayed,*
> *for I am thy God, and will still give thee aid;*
> *I'll strengthen thee, help thee, and cause thee to stand,*
> *upheld by my righteous, omnipotent hand.*
>   —"HOW FIRM A FOUNDATION," ATTRIBUTED TO ROBERT KEENE OR GEORGE KEITH, 1787

I once saw a mama bear walking four of her babies while I was at a camp and my two oldest daughters were still quite young. The cubs looked like actual teddy bears, and the mama seemed amused, yet aware.

With my girls pressed tight against my side, we stood still and silent and watched them frolic together until slowly they moved on down the hill and out of view.

The encounter was awesome in the truest sense. It was a majestic sight, yet my heart was racing from the danger that had just walked across our path. I knew that as playful and present as the mama was with her bear cubs, she would be just as powerful and protective if she sensed my girls too near or thought we might have been a danger.

The cubs, safe under their mother's protection and gentle guidance, seemed to be having the time of their lives.

T. G. Steward's one simple song said to "Praise the Lord for He is just" in an unjust world.

For the children of God, His righteousness and judgment is not a threat to us, but a kindness. Like the cubs, we are free to enjoy the world and the love of our Father, safe under His ultimate protection and justice.

16.

Mercy

Freed us from the slavery
of th' invading enemy:
for His mercies shall endure,
ever faithful, ever sure.

—"LET US WITH A GLADSOME MIND," JOHN MILTON, 1623

KYRIE ELEISON IS A GREEK phrase meaning "Lord, have mercy." As long as Christians have needed forgiveness, these two words have been a part of our song.

Jesus told a parable of a tax collector whose head was too heavy from shame to even look up to heaven as he asked, "God, have mercy on me, a sinner." The man went home justified (Luke 18:13–14). Two blind men called out, "Have mercy on us, Son of David!" Jesus touched their eyes and their sight was restored (Matt. 9:27–30). "For all those who exalt themselves will be humbled, and those who humble themselves will be exalted," Jesus reminded us in Luke 14:11.

Roman Catholics, Anglicans, and the Eastern Orthodox Church—the Beatles, Rolling Stones, and Beach Boys of the liturgical world—almost always have a part of their service called The

Kyrie. It's a simple plea for penance to God the Father, Christ the Son, and the Holy Spirit.

Kyrie Eleison
Christe Eleison
Kyrie Eleison

Lord, have mercy
Christ, have mercy
Lord, have mercy

Sung, spoken, or chanted, this simple acknowledgment of our need, with no caveats or excuses, can be traced back almost to the very beginning of the Christian church itself. The phrase spread across the Roman Empire and can be found in the writings of Augustine in the Western Church of Algeria and Africa and in those of John of Constantinople, in the Greek-speaking East.[8]

Not only did the *Kyrie Eleison* survive both sides of the Great Schism between the Eastern Orthodox and Roman Catholic Church in 1054, but this simple hymn and prayer would live on to flourish at both ends of Martin Luther's Reformation as well.

As long as that song has been around, there is an older song still. Most likely written by King David (clearly the Bible's Elvis if we're following the rock and roll metaphor), Psalm 136 would have been written a thousand years before the birth of Jesus, and its final form as a song was probably settled a few hundred years after that, so people have been singing it for a long, long time.

It's a call and response song, where someone would sing out a line saying something about who God is or what He's done, and then everyone would respond "His mercy endures forever."

Look up Psalm 136 in different English translations, and you will actually find many different variations for the wording of the response that happens over and over.[9] Some of these are:

> *His love endures forever.*
> *For His steadfast love endures forever.*
> *For His faithful love lasts forever.*
> *For His faithfulness is everlasting.*
> *God's love never fails.*
> *For His lovingkindness is everlasting.*
> *For His mercy endures forever.*

You know what this tells me?

The English language is no match for the widths and depths of the love and mercy God has for us.

A few years ago, I was asked to lead worship at a friend's church. The sermon was about mercy. I went to choose songs based on the topic and, to my surprise, the list was much thinner than I anticipated.

We don't sing chants or short songs in most churches these days, so most of us have lost the heritage of such sacred phrases as the *Kyrie Eleison*. Worship leaders want to be encouraging and keep the energy up, so they tend to choose songs about feeling loved and safe and how God makes us feel, how great God is, and how we're going to praise Him. All good things!

Yet it becomes very easy, when our services don't have something like the *Kyrie* built in, to slowly sing less about our sin and our need (it doesn't feel very encouraging, after all), and thus sing less about what God has done for us, how we've been forgiven, how we ought to forgive others.

I've heard it said that as we grow deeper in our faith, we are also becoming more aware of our sin, and the closer we grow to God.

Even the very best of us will never outgrow our need for mercy, or for repeating this prayer weekly, nightly, daily.

How to Remember

Lord, have mercy
Christ, have mercy
Lord, have mercy

Father, give us mercy from the evil that has been done to us.
Jesus, give us mercy for the harm that we have done to others.
Spirit, give us mercy from the darkness that stirs without end inside our own hearts.

—KYRIE ELEISON

17.

Forgiveness

> There's a wideness in God's mercy,
> like the wideness of the sea.
> There's a kindness in God's justice,
> which is more than liberty.
>
> For the love of God is broader
> than the measures of the mind,
> and the heart of the Eternal
> is most wonderfully kind.
>
> —"THERE'S A WIDENESS IN GOD'S MERCY," FREDERICK WILLIAM FABER, 1862

LIKE A CHERISHED FAMILY RECIPE, the mercy we have tasted is meant to be shared.

For me, it started at a Pizza Hut lunch buffet. I was probably twenty-three years old and pretty bitter about the way some business dealings had gone. Truthfully, in hindsight, I was probably to blame for most of the issue in the first place, but I was too young and proud to admit that, or even understand it, at the time.

There I was, an unemployed newlywed, scared out of my mind and just angry at the world for not playing by the rules I had assumed existed. I had been the good kid. The church guy. The nice boy who did the right things most of the time (at least in public), and who expected God and the world to give him what he was due.

If there was a character like me in the Bible it wasn't the prodigal son, but his older brother. I was a Pharisee. I'd never understood why these guys always seemed so angry, but I get it now. The internal rage of the self-righteous, who cannot stand it when somebody cuts in front of the line they've been standing in their entire life.

I also get why nobody seemed to want to be around them. They don't sound like a lot of fun.

Thankfully, I had a friend like Matthew.

I hope at some point you have one like him too. He invited me out to lunch and we chatted for a while, and then he kind of worked the conversation around to this one particular businessperson I had blamed for a lot of my angst and frustration.

He listened as I went through my rant about how awful that guy was and, once I'd finally worn myself out and hit a lull, Matthew took a deep breath and said, "I asked you to lunch to tell you something that I think the rest of our friends are too scared to tell you."

He looked me straight in the eye.

"You're a jerk."

Actually, my good Christian publishers won't allow me to print what he really said, but your imagination can do the trick.

"Excuse me?" I said.

He repeated himself.

Then he asked me a question.

"Have you ever thought about forgiving him?"

No, my friends, I had not. Not even a little bit.

In fact, when Matthew said the word "forgiving" I genuinely felt as if I had never even heard that word before anywhere in my experience of the English language.

I don't remember the rest of the conversation, but I know that I snot-cried in a Pizza Hut. I eventually did forgive that business guy. And something started to change for this guy too.

It happened slowly. Good things usually do. Years later, I was not a perfect person, but I can say, and all my friends would say as well, that I am not that bitter, angry man I was at age twenty-three. Forgiveness changes us.

Forgiveness doesn't mean everything gets better. It doesn't close up a wound or erase the memory of what happened.

No, it is the conscious and continual choice to let go of your right to condemn someone for the ways that they've harmed you. It is choosing to set down the anger, to fully feel the pain, and to start to walk toward your own healing, regardless of what was done to you.

The ancient Hebrew prayers of repentance contain multiple words for forgiveness, each meaning slightly different things: paying off a debt or commuting a punishment, a complete writing off of negative consequences for a harmful action, or the reconciliation of a relationship between the offender and the victim.

Note that many types of forgiveness do not involve making things right between two people. Sometimes this is not possible, as one party is not willing, unavailable, or worse. Sometimes this could even be dangerous, unsafe, or unwise. God is, mercifully, always open to relationship with the vilest abuser, but that does not at all mean that the ones they've abused need to be. (That's not the point of this chapter, by the way, it just needs to be said.)

Here *is* the point:

The heart of God is kind.

I did not always know this.

When you've been introduced to God as an angry cop, a distant relative, or a vicious warrior, as many of us have been, it should be no surprise when some of our first instincts are not to seek shelter *in* Him, but *from* Him.

Yet God seeks to find places where our guard is down and will continue to show up in the strangest and most humble circumstances to meet with us. Until, one day, we at last discover God's heart, as our eyes finally follow the lonely and winding pathway, up a hillside thick with mockers, where Jesus laid His life down for us, His friends.

> *Amazing love! how can it be*
> *That Thou, my God, should die for me!*
> *No condemnation now I dread;*
> *Jesus, and all in Him is mine!*
> —"AND CAN IT BE," CHARLES WESLEY, 1738

I am a man who has been forgiven so many times. By God, yes, but also by my wife, my parents, my friends, my colleagues, and maybe the most humbling of all, my children.

Being forgiven has changed me. Kindness has taught me more than lectures or punishment ever could. It's showed me not simply where I'm wrong, but what other choices are possible for me and the bigger story God has created for me. It takes my focus off defending myself so that I can have eyes and vision for what I can do for others.

Forgiveness has invited me into a bigger life.

There's a harmony to this melody, of course. I've had to forgive a lot too.

I've not always been very good at it. I can hold a grudge like a hand grenade. I'll slide that thing into my pocket and just keep it there all day where nobody else can see it. It gives me a sense of power, of control, of feeling better than somebody else.

This is why I, personally, get sucked into politics again and again. It feels really satisfying to have some villains in my life, people who are so clearly wrong (in my opinion) who I can look down on with disdain and self-righteousness, especially on days when my own failures and shortcomings are ganging up on me.

Good old human nature.

In wanting to feel a little more powerful, I just make myself smaller. I slide further back into my selfishness and arrogance. Holding on to anger always turns to bitterness, and bitterness never looked good on anybody. It's a nasty thing.

I could never return the favor and forgive as much as I have been forgiven, but I did forgive that music business guy. I've forgiven politicians I've never met. I've had to forgive my parents, my friends, my wife, people I work with, people in traffic, the government of the state of Tennessee (there I go again), and the list goes on. Sometimes it's a simple deep breath and a shake of the head, and other times it's years of work and prayer and walks in the woods.

If it took Jesus dying to forgive me, well, I shouldn't expect it to be easy for me to forgive another.

. . . especially not myself.

I'm still working on that one.

For now, I'll stand under the rain of His mercy there and pray that it waters the seeds of my own.

Every drop I have tasted of forgiveness has been so, so good.

Being forgiven has changed my life, unlocking my chains. Forgiving others has opened the prison doors, actually setting *me* free.

If we did not have Jesus, bitterness and spite are really all we would have left. What a mercy it is, what kindness, that the cross has made forgiveness possible. Not just between God and us, but flowing downhill, giving us the choice and the freedom to forgive one another as well.

18.

Otherness

Heaven and earth are full of the Majesty of Thy Glory.
The Holy Church throughout all the world doth acknowledge Thee.
The Father of an infinite Majesty;
Also the Holy Ghost, the Comforter.
Thou art the everlasting Son of the Father.
When thou tookest upon Thee to deliver man,
Thou didst not abhor the Virgin's womb.
—"TE DEUM LAUDAMUS," AMBROSE OR NICETAS, BISHOP OF REMESIANA, FOURTH CENTURY

WHEN I WAS PROBABLY SEVEN years old, I started having panic attacks at night. I could not sleep. I would run out of my room, shaking, to find my parents.

My Sunday school teachers had been describing the eternal nature of God. "That means He lives forever," they would tell me. "Imagine your life is a line that has a beginning and an end. But God's life is a circle; it just keeps going and going. No beginning, no end."

It freaked me *all* the way out. Honestly, just writing it out now sends a shiver down my spine and makes me want to go do something else.

I liked hearing about Noah and the animals and Jesus and miracles, but God and time was too much for me.

It might have been too much for the fundamentalism I grew up with too. God, I was told, was strong and powerful, yet the list of things that He would and wouldn't do was stark and rigid. God liked this and hated that. Of these things we were certain, and that was comforting.

Years later, in my early twenties, I was now living in a big city on my own. The certainty had gone, and with it, the comfort. I'd learned enough to ask questions of everything, but not enough to have confidence in anything.

Like many young men looking for answers, I decided, with a shallow understanding of Calvinism, that God had chosen me from before the beginning of time to let everyone else know why they were wrong and I . . . sorry, God . . . was right. Misreading the intricacies of this worldview for a black-and-white system that could save from the doubt I was drowning in, I stepped into a different world from that of my upbringing with different ideas about God, but where the rules were just as rigid, and again I could be certain and comforted in them.

If you've ever met those young men—or, like me and my friends, *been* them—you know how fun it is to hang out with someone who has complete confidence in how everything works about God and life and is *more* than happy to explain it to you.

Of course, I had simply traded one fundamentalism for another. Looking around, I see this everywhere. Politics, identities, fad diets . . . People skitter in a panic from one extreme ideology to another, trying to find a way to make the world make sense.

But the world won't ever make sense. It's too big, too wild, too out of control. There are too many gravitational forces pulling in too many directions at the same time. So many people trying to get more than they need, all fueled by inner ids and egos and who knows what else that they don't understand themselves—let alone understand anyone else.

All this atop only one of the sinning, spinning, bustling, breathtaking, orbiting balls of basalt and granite hurtling through space in the universe that God created and called "good."

How could we ever hope to understand the holy mind of such a maker?

> *In the beginning was the Word, and the Word was with God, and the Word was God. He was with God in the beginning. Through him all things were made; without him nothing was made that has been made. In him was life, and that life was the light of all mankind. The light shines in the darkness, and the darkness has not overcome it. (John 1:1–5)*

That's beautiful. Inspiring. And also . . . not a science textbook. This passage invites questions. People introduce each other with information. "Hi, I'm Chaunda and I work in data systems and I have two cats." God is being described here as poetry through poetry. His introduction is invitation to mystery and curiosity.

God is other.

To be "other" in this sacred sense is what we call "holy." Set apart. Completely and utterly different from this world and all that is in it.

> *In the beginning God created the heavens and the earth. Now the earth was formless and empty, darkness was over the surface of the deep, and the Spirit of God was hovering over the waters. (Gen. 1:1–2)*

Jesus came to earth and suffered and died to save us and befriend us and relate to us as a human in the flesh. I do not relate to this part of God at all. Hovering over the water before the creation of the world is not a metaphor that correlates with my life. He is simply *other*.

Further down in verse 26, God says, "Let us make mankind in our image."

Our. God the Father, God the Son, God the Spirit. The Trinity.

What is more "other" than a being, creating things out of nothing, existing outside of time and space in a perfect, harmonious relationship with three different people who are Himself?

God is other.

You're likely familiar with "Holy, Holy, Holy," one of the most well-known and wonderful hymns of the past hundred years, which is all about this otherness.

> *Holy, holy, holy,*
> *Merciful and mighty,*
> *God in three Persons, blessed Trinity!*
> —"HOLY, HOLY, HOLY," REGINALD HEBER, 1826

Songs of this era, like that of most generations before us, were not scared to get into the poetry or supernatural realm of the Bible with its unfamiliar words and ideas that could make us at times feel a little discomforted. In fact, in the next verse, Reginald Heber, the songwriter, starts literally naming the kinds of angels that are listed in the book of Revelation.

> *Cherubim and seraphim, falling down before Thee,*
> *who was and is and evermore shall be.*

Finally, Heber brings our own human lens to the conversation. Like the sun behind a cloud, the veil of doubt and the weight of sin that keep us from experiencing the full weight of the glory of God does not make it shine any less bright. It only dulls our perception, for a moment.

> *Holy, holy, holy,*
> *though the darkness hide Thee,*
> *though the eye of sinful man Thy glory may not see;*
> *only Thou art holy, there is none beside Thee*
> *Perfect in power, in love and purity.*

This hymn was not an anomaly. Christians have been singing songs like this for hundreds of years. This one is from Ambrose of Milan in the fourth century, titled, "O Lux Beata Trinitas."

> *O Trinity, most blessed light,*
> *O Unity of sov'reign might,*
> *as now the fiery sun departs,*
> *come shed your light within our hearts.*

You know when you go out hiking and you want to take a picture of the giant, open sky and the wide, yawning valley below? You pull up your phone to see what those miles of vista look like on a 4 x 2-inch screen and you are reminded of what it's like to be human in a world inhabited by a supernatural Creator. No way can we fit Him in the frame of our camera.

Yet, as with so many things we keep discovering about God, while His otherness operates on this vast, universal level on one hand, on the other He is with us in the mud and clay and the heartache and the molecules that make up our daily existences.

When God's people were enslaved in Egypt and after they left, He was doing miracles. And it could get weird.

Water turned to blood. Frogs fell from the sky. The sun went dark. He split the sea, then closed it on the enemy's army.

God is other.

Flip to the New Testament and here comes Jesus, turning water into wine. In the middle of the lake walking across the water, freaking His friends out. The blind can see. The dead are waking up. An insane man is now normal, while the pigs next to him run into the lake and drown themselves.

God is other.

I heard stories when I was in India that sounded straight out of those Gospels. Healings, possessions, all sorts of miracles. Have we in the West made the mistake of thinking that science and the supernatural are opposites, rather than dance partners? Are we missing things right in front of our faces? Have we let this blade of our faith get too dull?

Yet, I have friends who speak in tongues. Who have seen things in dreams. That's not me, but when I was eighteen, I was in a car crash and a man immediately came to my window, knew just what to do, unhooked the battery, helped me out of the wreckage, and vanished before any other cars came on the scene. Who was that guy? I've always wondered. Did he have wings under that flannel shirt? I don't know, man. I don't know.

What I do know is that if God was faithful in strange and holy ways before, and He's planning on that in the future, then He is very likely doing that kind of thing right now, whatever that might mean or look like.

We can't understand it or control it and, like a seven-year-old scared in the middle of the night, that can be overwhelming. Yet there is a surreal comfort, a "peace that passes understanding," that who we can't control or hope to understand is faithfully and mysteriously working for our good.

HONORABLE MENTIONS

As I said before, this book is not a scientific study of hymns, nor a college textbook describing all the types of songs churches have ever sung anywhere at any time. I'm just a guy who probably pays more attention than most to what we sing and what we don't.

What I have learned, though, is that what we sing about God, and what we don't, shapes us like a river carving a landscape. It is of incredible importance.

In the hymnbooks on my shelf, I found that hymns of previous generations overwhelmingly sang of suffering, doubt, time, place, and peace in ways we typically do not. They also sang about the mysteries of God—His presence, glory, righteousness, mercy, forgiveness, and otherness—with courage and reverence that we largely avoid today.

However, I'm pretty sure that comparing hymnals from the past 150 years and today's roster of Christian hits still leaves out a *vast* expanse of church history and worldwide experience. Nowhere on today's list are there songs of persecution, an experience familiar to much of the church throughout time including the present; or songs about poverty, also a common Christian circumstance; nor did I touch on topics like obedience, giving, fasting, or feasting, which also have a rich history of songs worth celebrating, and more importantly, worth singing.

As with anything in the kingdom of God, there is always so much more to discover.

However, there are three themes I don't see prevalent in either the hymnals on my shelf or during Sunday mornings now that I'd like to explore more here:

Songs of Exodus, Stories of Jesus, and Songs of Scripture.

19.

Songs of Exodus

Oh, don't you want to go to that gospel feast,
That promised land where all is peace?
Oh, deep river, Lord,
I want to cross over.

—"DEEP RIVER" IS A TRADITIONAL NEGRO SPIRITUAL

SEVENTH GRADE IS ROUGH.

If you know someone who absolutely loved seventh grade, you also know a lot of people who don't like that person.

You are fully aware of yourself and your place in the social order. You know exactly what you aren't wearing that everyone else is. What you don't have that everyone else has. What you can't do that everyone else can.

And because seventh graders are so insecure about their own deficiencies, they can be very quick to point out everyone else's.

When you're in seventh grade, it's the oldest you've ever been. You have no experience being any older, you can't really imagine it and, without ever saying it out loud, it just seems like this is your life now, and it will be like this forever.

I have dropped all three of my daughters off at the gates of that lion's den, and it is the most powerless feeling in the world.

Our youngest daughter, Charlotte, is an amazing kid. She is riotously funny, fiercely compassionate, and a deep thinker. She loves to write and sing and can read the same book ten times over, finding something new in it every time. She lives with her eyes wide open. Amazing traits that unfortunately make you extra aware of your middle school experience.

Third kids get a lot of leftovers and hand-me-downs, but they also get parents who have actually done this before, so it was not until dropping Charlotte off that I finally had the experience to say:

"Okay, here's the deal: Seventh grade is a lot of things. There will be days that are incredibly hard, and days where this is really fun! Whatever the day is, it will not last forever. Each day will end and you get to come back home."

"See all these girls," I continued, pointing at the green-skirted students making their way up the sidewalk. "You are all in a boat together, floating down the same river. Rainy days, sunny days, still water or rapids. It doesn't actually matter what anybody's wearing. You're all on a journey you didn't ask for, but you're together, and someday you will all get out of the boat together too. If you can remember this, it will help you savor the good days and get through the hard ones. You've got this!"

To be honest, I don't know if this was the advice she needed to hear, or that I was trying to send down some magical, Styrofoam cup phone line back through time to when I thought I was trapped in a lonely year that I thought would never end myself.

One of my favorite hymnals in my collection is full of Negro spirituals, handed down from people who were enslaved on plantations. They are usually built around multiple repetitions, substituting one word or phrase with each new verse. These were mostly simple songs, rarely written down until much later.

Contrary to our modern worship catalog, the core of these songs is mourning (for good reason), and what joy we hear is based in hope for the future. These words are from "Soon-a Will Be Done":

> Soon-a will be done-a with the troubles of the world.
> Goin' home to live with God.
> No more weeping and a-wailing,
> I'm goin' to live with God.

These songs hold little mention of how God's love makes us feel. They are songs of exodus, of people who *know* that they are not home, but are holding on to hope that they will be there one day.

There are moments where my grief or pain can resonate on these frequencies. I can feel the ache and longing in my bones. (The older I get, the more naturally this comes.) When I am hanging out, grilling burgers, and playing campfire songs with my friends, though, not so much.

We exist in a unique place on the timeline of human geography. By that I mean, ours is one of the only cultures in the history of the world that has not lived with the expectation of pain and difficulty.

Here in the modern West, we view trial as an exception.

Washing machines, fast food, Wi-Fi, and office jobs have removed us from the long, hard drudgery our ancestors went through just to stay alive. In many ways, this is a gift and a mercy. But watch out. Trouble must be around the corner for anyone getting too comfortable in a place that is, in the end, deeply *un*-comfortable.

God is not trying to keep this a secret from us.

How to Remember

One of the books in the Bible is called Exodus, meaning "a departure of a large group of people." It feels like almost every other page in the rest of the Bible references this. The story of the Israelites, God's chosen people, wandering through the desert on the way to their promised homeland, ends up being one of the biggest stories of the Old Testament, if not the whole Bible.

The spiritual "Go Down Moses" sings of this:

> *When Israel was in Egypt's land,*
> *Let my people go,*
> *oppressed so hard they could not stand,*
> *Let my people go.*
>
> *Go down, Moses, way down in Egypt's land,*
> *tell old Pharaoh: Let my people go.*

When Jesus was born, His parents soon had to take Him and hide in another country, as the king, who was threatened by rumors of the birth of the Messiah, was having all the baby boys in the region put to death.

Years later, when He had begun His ministry, a scribe said he wanted to follow Him. Jesus replied with this cryptic line: "Foxes have dens and birds have nests, but the Son of Man has no place to lay his head" (Luke 9:58). In His ministry, He traveled from town to town and wanted the scribe to understand that following Jesus was signing up for an altogether different kind of life. Pledging a new allegiance to a new citizenship.

Deep down, even in our comfort, our transformed hearts understand this too. We feel the push of one world and the pull of the next, and we know we don't belong here.

The endless scroll of our phones is telling us there is more. The constant grind to achieve is telling us there must be rest. The knowledge that we will all die will either give us utter terror or sweet hope that there is life, and life more abundantly than any we have yet seen or experienced.

Just like seventh grade is not forever, this life, as it is right now, is not our home.

> *On Jordan's stormy banks I stand,*
> *and cast a wishful eye*
> *to Canaan's fair and happy land,*
> *where my possessions lie.*
> *I am bound for the promised land.*
> —"ON JORDAN'S STORMY BANKS I STAND," SAMUEL STENNETT, 1787

Does this change how we think and pray and go about our days? What we prioritize and how we treat the homeless and the environment and the voting booth? Does it change the way we practice our faith and the songs we sing?

If we want to be like Christ, are we willing to live in the reality that we are pilgrims? Foreigners in a foreign land. God's chosen people, homesick for a new heaven and a new earth.

Could we sing again the songs of exodus?

20.

Stories of Jesus

Zacchaeus was a wee little man
A wee little man was he
He climbed up in a sycamore tree
For the Lord he wanted to see

And when the Savior passed that way
He looked up in the tree
And He said: "Zacchaeus, you come down!
For I'm going to your house today!"
—(AMERICAN FOLK SONG)

HAVE YOU EVER RUN INTO someone you think you're friends with, and midway through the conversation you realize that you've never actually met them before? It turns out you just have a lot of mutual connections and have heard so many stories about each other that you just kind of think you know each other.

In a way, maybe you do.

When you want to get to know someone, you go out to dinner or you go for a walk and you tell each other stories. You talk about where you grew up, who your family is, or where you went to school and the crazy things that happened to you there. You ask questions about who your friends are, what you do for work, and you learn about each other's hobbies and the things you're both passionate about.

Even if you've not sat with someone directly, if you've heard someone's stories enough even indirectly, you do sort of know them.

That's the strange thing about having a public persona, even the teeniest tiniest bit that I do as an indie Christian musician. People have listened to my music for decades, come to my shows, streamed my podcast. They've spent hundreds of hours hearing my stories and they have a sort of relationship with me that, unfortunately, and sometimes awkwardly, I'm not able to reciprocate.

Jesus, on the other hand, does know our stories. He knows our longings and our fears. Our hearts and our shame. He is cheering on our victories!

We're the ones who need to hear *His* stories.

When I suggest we should sing songs about the stories of the life of Jesus, most people assume I am talking about singing children's songs. To be fair, I'm not *not* talking about that. It's wonderful that children are singing those songs! We can learn many things from our children, and this is surely one of them.

What if we sang more songs that simply retold the stories of Jesus we read in the Bible? About the things He did, the things He said, the people He cared about? What a great way to get to know Him!

You see, sometimes our songs about Jesus can be so full of metaphors and insider spiritual language that it's almost like a friend describing a blind date in a movie. "You would love Jesus. He has such a great personality, a wonderful sense of humor. He loves children. He's an ocean."

If you were to walk into a church off the street not knowing much about Jesus, then, many of our songs about Him might not make a lot of sense to you. Truthfully, I am quite guilty of this as a songwriter. I love metaphors and I have grown up with the Bible and, if I'm not careful, I can easily end up writing songs with the assumption that everybody knows these stories as well as I do.

But a lot of people don't.

To use poetic or powerful words about Him is wonderful, but to tell the real stories of what He did and the way He actually changed people's lives, and even the strange things He did and said, is maybe, at times, even better.

Recently I had the chance to sit with a man who works in Indonesia, teaching songwriting and capturing field recordings of native tribes who have recently converted to Christianity. First generation Christians. No music business. No megachurches. Just real life, tangible transformation.

I got to listen to several songs from these villages. They were the first songs about Jesus ever written in that language. It was hard to see the translations on his computer screen through the tears in my eyes.

Most of the songs were just voices and drums. Some of them were twenty minutes long with the same melody the entire time. Structurally, sonically, culturally—in every way—they were foreign, yet the story was familiar.

If you walked in off the street not knowing anything about Jesus and you heard that song, by the end of it, you would know exactly who Jesus was and what He did. The songs were so beautiful in their poetic simplicity.

The song that truly wrecked me was this one, called "Ke Aidogha Muna."[10] It's a lament by Robi Waramori. Here's the English translation:

> *Because of the sins of mankind, the Lord Jesus died for us.*
> *Judas betrayed him; he sold the Lord Jesus.*
> *Gethsemane was where the Lord was captured.*
> *The place was the beginning of the suffering of the Lord Jesus.*
> *His mother Mary remembered her son; she cried because of his goodness.*
> *The Lord Jesus bore his burden; he bore his burden, our burden.*
> *He bore his burden, our burden; our burden of sin, our sins.*
> *His holy blood poured out on the earth forgave sins, the sins of the world.*
> *He was hung on a cross; hung on the hill of Golgotha.*
> *Our Lord, our great Lord; our great Lord, the Lord God.*
> *You love your people; because of your love, we are saved.*

I recognize this same kind of unadorned clarity, not in the flowery eloquence of Luther and Watts and the European hymn-writers, but in the words of many spirituals.

"Were you there when they crucified my Lord?" one famous unattributed song asks.

> *Oh, sometimes it causes me to tremble, tremble, tremble.*
> *Were you there when they nailed him to the tree?*
> *Were you there when they laid him in the tomb?*
> *Were you there when God raised him from the tomb?*

There are many ways to tell a story—some more narrative-driven than others—but if we come to know people by sharing our histories, then the more we share the stories of Jesus, the better we will come to know Him.

21.

Songs of Scripture

*The Word of God is a Tree of Life
That offers its fruit to all who hunger.
Its branches extend over the earth,
Feeding those who draw near in faith.*

—EPHREM THE SYRIAN, AD 303–373

KEITH AND KRISTYN GETTY HAVE become known around the world for their songwriting and work in promoting modern hymns. Keith also, like me, has a house full of daughters, who happen to go to school with mine, and we have become friends, both as guys who care about sacred songs and as girl dads at school things.

He is always dropping little nuggets of brilliance in conversation, but I actually read this quote randomly in an interview he gave to *American Songwriter* magazine a couple years ago:

"Twenty percent of Scripture is actually songs and poetry. In other words, the God of the Bible actually creates us in a way that we need songs, we need poems."[11]

You can always trust an Irishman to cut right to the point.

We spend so much of our time in the modern American church

referencing Scripture or borrowing ideas from Scripture for our songs that it's easy to forget that so much of it is actually already song. It's literally built to be sung.

For most of human history, people did not have a printed Bible sitting on their shelf. Scriptures were sung to teach and learn and invite its messages to inhabit hearts and minds.

In the past few generations, we have thought of singing Scripture as mainly a tool to teach children, and children only. We tend to think of these compositions as kids' songs. We give them childish melodies.

Yet there have been a handful of songs that slipped through to a wider audience. One of my very favorite worship songs since high school has been "Create in Me a Clean Heart," which I did not realize until many years later was a direct paraphrase of a passage from Psalm 51:10–12 (ESV).

> *Create in me a clean heart, O God,*
> *and renew a right spirit within me.*
> *Cast me not away from your presence,*
> *and take not your Holy Spirit from me.*
> *Restore to me the joy of your salvation,*
> *and uphold me with a willing spirit.*

The song was originally recorded by Keith Green and written by Brown Bannister, a legendary record producer who spends most of his time these days as a friend and mentor to many of us songwriters and artists in the generations behind him. It's fun to connect the dots now, but at the time the song just seemed to appear one day on an overhead sheet with chords Sharpied over the words, projected on the wall for our youth group—I didn't know for thirty years who wrote or recorded it—which I'm sure is exactly how Brown and Keith would want it.

I cannot tell you how many times in my life that song has popped into my head. In different seasons I have needed various sections of it. Every single line has been vital at some point, which should not be a surprise.

It's Scripture. It's simply doing its job.

> For the word of God is alive and active. Sharper than any double-edged sword, it penetrates even to dividing soul and spirit, joints and marrow; it judges the thoughts and attitudes of the heart. (Heb. 4:12)

You may notice that a lot of the songs and hymns I reference in this book are from European cultures; some of that is because we obviously share a root language, and technology allowed for records to be preserved better after a certain point, for sure. The more I look and learn, though, the more I find that many cultures weren't singing songs referencing or responding to Scripture, but they were focused on finding new ways to sing Scripture itself. There simply aren't as many "other" songs from those cultures to even quote!

There are parts of the Bible that we might find terribly boring, like genealogies for instance; yet people have sung them. The stories of the Old Testament, macro like the Israelites fleeing Egypt or micro like Samuel hearing the voice of the Lord in the middle of the night—people have sung them. The miracles of Jesus or the prophecies of Revelation—people have sung them.

The Bible is wide, wild, and surprising. As deep as you want to swim, there is ocean to explore.

Wonderfully, people singing Scripture is not just left in the past, nor is it isolated in hidden cultural cul-de-sacs. Artists, projects, and even small movements all around the country are carrying on this rich tradition still today.

I've had the privilege of working with or befriending a few of them—like Randall Goodgame's *Scripture Hymnal*, the indie-rock Verses collective out of Colorado, and Birmingham's The Corner Room, but these barely scratch the surface. A quick internet search will turn up incredible music from Psallos, Living Water, Every Last Word, Seeds, The Psalms Project and a seemingly infinite number of other believers bringing their own melodies of the Bible to the choir. Some of my favorite songs from the Anchor Hymns community I lead have been Scripture set to music as well.

I'll be honest. I wish more of these made their way into Sunday morning services.

It is no secret that biblical literacy among American Christians has been on a steep decline for years. Overall, we just don't read as much as we used to in general, and we don't read the Bible as much either. But not knowing the Bible makes it harder for us to know God. When we have questions or doubts, which are natural and human, it's harder for us to know what to do with them.

Learning Scripture through song is a simple and beautiful way of inviting God's Word to move from our lips to our heart and on into our very bone and marrow.

MARROW

I used to find it boring
these ancient words on a Sunday
said over and over
week after week

Until one Thursday
in the plumbing aisle at Home Depot
I was surprised to find
the words were still there
breeding in my marrow
sailing through my veins
another colored blood cell,
red, white and true

Taxes are boring
but roads and schools and hospitals
are good, not just for me
but for us
the friends, the family
the aliens, the enemies

So lay the words on my lips
let me taste them on my tongue
that I might recognize them in my heart's beat

Until it stops

22.

Liturgies

A DIGRESSION

I GO TO A "LITURGICAL" church. That means we follow an order of service that is written down, and you can follow along.

If you go to church of any kind, you likely have an order to your service as well. (Which, in essence, means *all* churches are liturgical!)

A liturgy is simply that: an order of service. The way you structure your time together, the way you've traditionally done things—this is your liturgy. Some have been created more intentionally than others.

There are as many different ways to worship God as there are human beings made in His image. Over the years, some of those image bearers have crafted words and thought into structures of sequence and symbol to help other believers enter into deeper communion with Christ.

Today's megachurches are no different. Theirs is a unique contribution to the history of the church, with its screens and its backing tracks and satellite campuses. Some of these are helpful, some debatable. Time will likely be the judge.

As I've traveled around the world and met so many different Christians and experienced the different ways they worship and structure their corporate times together, I am less and less convinced that there is a right or wrong way to do it. All God asks is for a humble heart that seeks Him in spirit and in truth. I don't think He cares if you're wearing board shorts or a three-piece suit. I don't think He cares if you're jumping and shouting or chanting in Latin.

I do think there is real beauty in the jumping and shouting *and* in the chanting in Latin, and that they can both learn from each other.

In any gathering for worship, outside of listening to a teacher, there are three things we do together as a group: sing, speak, and act.

We've explored many of the types of songs churches have historically sung. Now let's turn our gaze toward similarly overlooked prayers and practices, beginning with Sunday morning liturgies, through ancient symbols and practices, that eventually flow into the life and community of the church family. It's a fascinating journey, and one where we get to joyfully celebrate some growing signs of a dawning spring.

Again, I want to remind you that I'm here as a guide, not an expert. I'm a friend who wants to show you what has been so transformational in my own life, because I think you might find it helpful in yours. What you'll read here are not exhaustive research papers, but my personal experiences, reflections (and opinions), with some helpful information thrown in.

To start, let's dive into some of these older liturgies, particularly the words and prayers we speak together. In the tradition I was raised in, we rarely, if ever, spoke together aloud, yet I have learned that this is something highly valued in many Christian communities. I'd love to look at just a few of the ways Christ's followers can use their voices to speak together.

23.

The Lessons

So Ezra the priest brought the Law before the assembly, both men and women and all who could understand what they heard, on the first day of the seventh month. And he read from it facing the square before the Water Gate from early morning until midday, in the presence of the men and the women and those who could understand. And the ears of all the people were attentive to the Book of the Law. (Neh. 8:2–3 ESV)

"READ YOUR BIBLE AND PRAY every day."

I've always been told those are the keys to being a good Christian. One of those things (the Bible) even tells us to do the other thing (pray) "without ceasing" (1 Thess. 5:17 ESV).

Nowhere in Scripture, though, does Jesus say to read our Bibles every day. The people He was talking to actually couldn't, at least not the New Testament, which hadn't been written yet. They weren't reading about Jesus; they were actually going to hear Him speak when He came to the town nearby!

When Jesus went off to pray, as He so often did, He was not taking His copy of the NIV and His Moleskine notebook to journal.

What we know of now as the Old Testament was handed down first as oral tradition before finally being put down on paper (or parchment or scroll or whatever it may have been).[12] This is why so many of the earliest Bible stories, like creation, Cain and Abel, and Noah's ark follow the forms of poetry and narratives that were familiar to ancient Hebrew culture. They were the kinds of stories that were easily told and retold, generation to generation.

Eventually, though, they were codified, and to hear the official versions of the stories, not just the folk versions around the kitchen fires at night, people would go to the temple, where the priests would read aloud from a scroll of the sacred texts. Most people could not read at all, and would never be able to read the Scriptures for themselves, only hear them.

Keep in mind, there was no printing press. Reading and writing were not widely available to the masses, at least not in the form we think of now. To listen to the Scriptures was a sacred thing that happened at very specific times with utmost care. That scroll had been copied laboriously and meticulously by hand.

No one had a copy on their shelf.

Then, in 1440 in Mainz, Germany, Johannes Gutenberg invented the first movable type printing press in Europe, and suddenly, for the first time, books and other printed materials could be copied cheaply and quickly. Gutenberg's Bible, his first and most renowned project, began to be distributed, and a hundred years later there were printing presses and Bibles all around western Europe.

Now, five hundred years later, we have not only Bibles available in thousands of languages, but a wealth of different versions for English-readers that offer us slightly different cultural and contextual understandings of passages. It is now possible for people to have the Bible on their shelf at home, an amazing gift that Gutenberg gave to the world.

To be clear, too, I think reading the Bible every day is one of the greatest opportunities of the modern era, and now that it *is* possible, it's very good advice and we should not take it lightly.

It's only been the past couple hundred years that people have been able to have a Bible of their own, so not needing to hear it read to them as their main source to learn Scripture is a relatively new phenomenon. At the same time, there is something really special about hearing Scripture the way it was originally intended—read aloud to a group of people who have gathered to worship God and who hope to hear from Him.

Maybe you read Scripture aloud in your church each week. That's awesome!

Today, in most Catholic and liturgical traditions, Scripture is read like this:

1. An Old Testament passage—called the First Lesson or Reading

2. A responsive reading/singing/chanting of a psalm

3. A New Testament Reading—called the Second Lesson or Reading

4. Finally, a reading from one of the Gospels: Matthew, Mark, Luke, or John

I was asked to lead worship at a friend's church for a season where members with special needs took turns doing the Scripture reading before the sermon each week. Sometimes it took a while, and sometimes the individuals could be hard to understand. But the whole church learned the names and faces of that lovely and oft-forgotten group of people, and they learned some patience and humility too. It was beautiful.

I've been to churches where children offered Scripture readings, giving them a place to serve and be dignified. I've seen where verses were read while the megachurch worship band played, and the congregation took a moment, in that room of screens and fog machines, to sit under those sacred words together. It was wonderful.

Paul wrote in 1 Timothy 4:13: "Devote yourself to the public reading of Scripture, to preaching and to teaching" and, while that was a specific instruction for a specific time and place, I don't think that necessarily means it no longer applies. In an era where some of our church services are dominated by programming and personalities, uniting under the reading of Scripture takes the focus off of any celebrity or status or ambition and points it back to Christ.

There is no "right way" to read Scripture aloud on a Sunday morning, and about a million ways to imagine how it can enrich the time of worship and the lives of the people present in the room.

24.

Prayers in the Airport

"Popcorn style!"
"You dial, and I'll hang up."
"Brother Larry, would you bless this lunch for us?"
"Daddy God, we just, we just ask You, please don't let it rain during the Youth Group Car Washathon for Justice Mission Trip Explosion Fundraiser..."

WHEN I WAS TWENTY YEARS old, I missed a flight at Chicago's O'Hare airport.

I had to wait eight hours for the next flight out, just sitting around in the olden days before Wi-Fi or Netflix. I wandered in and out of a few overpriced bookstores and then heard over the loudspeaker an announcement for a "Catholic Mass in the airport chapel at three p.m."

How bored must a twenty-year-old kid be that going to a Mass in an airport seems entertaining? But I'd never been to any kind of Catholic service before, and I was kind of curious. Since I clearly had nothing better to do, I went.

The overhead fluorescents were on full blast, chasing away any shadow of mystery from the interfaith chapel, sterile and generic enough that it could have just hosted a luncheon for an elevator salesmen. The priest seemed more bored than I must have been to wander in in the first place, as he raced through the prayers and Scripture passages before getting to his next gig.

Yet something caught me. I was strangely drawn in. It was all so unfamiliar.

Or was it? Sitting there in a conference room chair with other stranded transients, I realized I recognized something.

Intention.

Even if the priest wasn't into it that day, the prayers were.

I've never liked jam bands, which might sound odd for a guitar player who really, really loves listening to great guitar players. But dudes playing notes just to play notes is not always that fun to listen to.

The great players, though, play with intention. Just like the lyrics of a great song or a novel or a play. There's a structure to it. A cadence, a kind of logic. Setting, conflict, resolution. A beginning, a middle, an end.

Though the priest was launching those prayers through the air like the jets outside the window, within them I recognized the same great writing that I loved in the songs of Springsteen or U2, or the beautiful compositions of Vivaldi and Beethoven that I had played in my high school orchestra.

I might not have been a very good songwriter yet, but I knew enough to know that being spontaneous is not the only form of being genuine, nor is it always the most honest.

The only kinds of prayer I had ever heard in my life had been jam bands. Everybody had been riffing. Some had played beautifully, some had missed a lot of notes, and some had just played scales over and over again, hoping no one noticed.

You learn, after a while, that sitting in to jam with people, unless they are really, really good, means just knowing a few of the right licks. In youth group, I knew how to say a few of the right phrases and sound like a genuine, deep, worshipful person, even in moments my heart was not in it at all. The fact that my prayer was "spontaneous" did not make it more or less genuine, nor was it really that spontaneous. I just played the licks I knew.

When you're given a piece of music that challenges you, it is humbling and daunting at first, but the skills you learn as you master that piece become tools you have to draw on when you compose your own music or find yourself in a setting where you have to improvise and, yes, get to sit in and jam. (Which sometimes is also really, really fun.)

There is no better teacher for a musician than to learn the music of better musicians.

Of course, we are not talking about music, we are talking about prayer. Prayer is not a skill or a performance; it is this mystical form of intimate, supernatural dialogue between God and humankind. It is talking and listening and revelation and silence and sometimes who knows what else.

Prayer is a thing we can be taught, and we also must discover. It is a thing meant for us, one on one, with God alone, and also for us as a body of believers, in one voice together.

We know prayer can be taught because Jesus taught us in Matthew 6:9–13: "This, then, is how you should pray," and then He said a short and simple prayer. It's one that is so profound and complete, so overwhelmingly *intentional* that it is still said around the world every day, everywhere from the Moscow Patriarchate to the Alcoholics Anonymous meeting in the Methodists' basement.

From as early as the second and third centuries, we see early Christian writers, like Hippolytus of Rome, writing forms of prayers for use during confession and the Eucharist. The fifth and sixth centuries saw St. Benedict and the rise of monastic thought. Many of the works created during that time are still in active use around the world to this day, like the Divine Office, also known as the Liturgy of the Hours. Of course, the book of Psalms was given to us even before Jesus walked onto the scene.

The Reformation led us to Thomas Cranmer, who compiled the *Book of Common Prayer*. Written in English rather than Latin, this volume provided Anglicans and Protestants with a handy volume of prayers, Scriptures and service orders for holidays, special occasions, and regular gatherings in the life of a worshiping church. For centuries, this book could be found in people's homes, and in the backs of church pews, between the Bible and the hymnal.

Many churches and traditions today still use that book, or a more contemporary version of it, as the framework for their Sunday morning services. It's only one traditional way of structuring a church's prayer life, though about 85 percent is straight from Scripture. When Jesus told us to pray as He did in the Lord's Prayer, He did not leave a step-by-step manual but gave us a framework. How we structure our services, and how we pray within them, whether off the cuff or from the page, that was not in His instructions.

One thing I have learned as a musician, and as a fan of so many other musicians, is that I deeply love both thoughtful, thoroughly intentional writing *and* brilliant, once-in-a-lifetime, spontaneous moments of inspiration. They are not in competition; rather they feed each other and make the experience of the other that much richer.

The same has been true with my experience of prayer. God has spoken to me, and listened to me, in deeply personal ways when I am yelling at the top of my lungs in my car and when I am standing with a group of songwriters reciting the thoughtfully crafted modern liturgies of my friend Doug McKelvey's book *Every Moment Holy*.

Years ago, my friend Stephen gave me a book by Walter Brueggemann. A legendary Old Testament scholar and professor, Brueggemann would apparently begin many of his Old Testament classes by praying over the students with a prayer he had written, based on his knowledge of the text he was about to teach and his relationship with those in the room. He thought little of these prayers afterward and would throw them away. To his students, though, they meant a great deal. They would often grab them out of trash baskets or slip them off his desk when he wasn't looking, to keep ones that were particularly meaningful.

Eventually, many of his students began to share with each other their secret keepsakes. The book I was given was a collection of those stolen treasures.[13]

Now almost anytime I lead a group of songwriters to write for the church, I read one of those prayers aloud to help set our course for the day.

The work we are doing is too important. Now is not the time to jam. If I'm going to lead these people well, I'm going to need to pray some well-written music.

25.

Confession / Absolution

> *May God our Father forgive us our sins*
> *and bring us to the eternal joy of his kingdom,*
> *where dust and ashes have no dominion.*
> *Amen.*
>
> (THE CHURCH OF ENGLAND, ABSOLUTION B 84)

CONFESSION IS MORE THAN ADMITTING guilt, though at times it is very much that. To confess is to admit your limitation. Your powerlessness. To stop acting like you've got it all together. To let out your stomach or stop hiding the limp.

We confess when we are caught and cornered, or when we can no longer bear the burden of the ruse, the shame.

But it is not enough to simply offer up the facts. Confession is a yin in search of a yang. It is a hand reaching out in the dark. And for what?

Absolution. Forgiveness for sin or wrongdoings; a release from our guilt, whether or not it releases us from the consequences.

Once we've realized we can't go on under the weight of truths untold, you would think we would rush to set them down, but so often, we don't. We will carry them for days, months, even years, unless we know, for certain, that mercy and kindness would be there for us when we do.

You see, we've been trained to expect the opposite. Too many times we've been caught and punished but not forgiven. Our faults have been revealed and we have been shamed, rather than loved.

Sometimes, yes, it's our pride or stubbornness that keeps us from confessing our sin, but many times, I wonder if it feels safer to continue in it than to risk the vulnerability of asking to be forgiven.

We had altar calls when I was a kid. *Come forward and commit your life to Jesus, or if you had "fallen away," come forward again and "rededicate your life" to Jesus!* There was some heavy-handed fire and brimstone involved that I'm okay to never experience again, though there is an aspect of the altar call, at least in theory, that's very beautiful. "Let the redeemed of the LORD tell their story," Psalm 107:2 says, and there are moments, just like in human relationships, where big public displays are necessary and appropriate.

The life of a relationship, however, is not in large public displays. It's a million small moments. A kind word. A loving touch. Taking out the garbage. Cleaning up the kitchen when you didn't make the mess.

Beneath the surface of those actions runs a teeming river of mercy in countless small choices. Choosing to prefer. Choosing to not be annoyed. Choosing to forgive.

These small moments of relationship create a rhythm of committing to one another, hurting each other, seeing and forgiving one another, and continuing to move forward in love and affection. This happens in all healthy relationships, whether the commitment is sealed on paper or not.

In looking at historic worship services, from the ancients through the *Book of Common Prayer* up to liturgical services of today, you find a similar quiet rhythm of relationship in the weekly sacred moments of confession and absolution.

This portion of the service typically follows a short, basic pattern. We take a few moments of silence together to confess our unworthiness and our sins to God. People are often given the option of kneeling or bowing during this time.

Then follows a prayer of confession. We acknowledge that we have fallen short of loving God and loving our neighbor. We affirm the goodness of God and ask for His forgiveness. We ask, too, in His mercy, for the strength to seek His will and that He would continue to lead us on the path of righteousness. This is our repentance.

These prayers can take many forms. Some are simple, some are longer and more complex. Some are direct:

> *Most merciful God,*
> *we confess that we have sinned against you*
> *in thought, word, and deed,*
> *by what we have done, and by what we have left undone.*
> *We have not loved you with our whole heart;*
> *we have not loved our neighbors as ourselves.*
> *We are truly sorry and we humbly repent.*
> *For the sake of your Son Jesus Christ,*
> *have mercy on us and forgive us;*
> *that we may delight in your will, and walk in your ways,*
> *to the glory of your Name.*
> *Amen.*[14]

And some more abstract:

> *We watch at a distance,*
> *and are slow to follow Christ in the way of the cross.*
> *Lord, have mercy.*
> **Lord, have mercy.**
>
> *We warm our hands by the fire,*
> *and are afraid to be counted among his disciples.*
> *Christ, have mercy.*
> **Christ, have mercy.**
>
> *We run away,*
> *and fail to share the pain of Christ's suffering.*
> *Lord, have mercy.*
> **Lord, have mercy.**[15]

Then follows a brief moment of reflection. Our guard is down, our secret mistakes and insecurities laid bare before the Lord. The hand reaches out.

Then the priest recites an Absolution. A powerful statement of Christ's mercy and redemption.

Again, this can take many forms, though it is traditionally very simple and clear.

> *Almighty God, our heavenly Father, who in his great mercy*
> *has promised forgiveness of sins to all those who sincerely*
> *repent and with true faith turn to him, have mercy upon*
> *you, pardon and deliver you from all your sins, confirm and*
> *strengthen you in all goodness, and bring you to everlasting*
> *life; through Jesus Christ our Lord. Amen.*[16]

Here is one from an older 1928 version of the *Book of Common*

Prayer that I particularly love:

> *The Almighty and Merciful Lord*
> *grant you absolution and remission of all your sins,*
> *true repentance,*
> *amendment of life,*
> *and the grace and consolation of his Holy Spirit.*
> **Amen.**[17]

That phrase "amendment of life" is so devastatingly powerful.

To be forgiven and absolved of our sins is wonderful, but for those of us who feel we've lost years to our sins, be it addiction, selfishness, or pride (or even worse—who have lost years to others' sin, who've been abused or abandoned), well . . . it can feel like having your credit cards paid off while you're stranded on a desert island. That's great, but I also need to get off this island.

"The almighty and merciful Lord grant you . . . time for amendment of life," the updated version of this statement says.[18] God does not promise to fix our earthly problems, but with the freedom we find in our repentance and forgiveness, we are now able to pursue healing in ways we could never have imagined. And we have "the grace and consolation of the Holy Spirit" with us, to comfort and guide us, whether our life is amended the way we'd like or not.

We may not get off the island in this life, but things have changed. We are not alone, and we will never be the same.

The hand that reaches out finds more than another hand in the dark. It is pulled into a full-body embrace and slowly led out of the darkness and into the light.

26.

Creeds

MY DAUGHTER SADIE LOVES HISTORY.

Our dinner conversations are often just the rest of us listening as she animatedly describes interesting facts about the past, like that President Andrew Jackson was given a 1,400-pound block of cheese that then sat in the White House entrance for two years, or that George Washington came to the Continental Congress dressed in a general's uniform every day until they finally just appointed him General. President Taft was so overweight he had custom bathtubs built for him everywhere he went, including on a cruise ship.

Also, the word for throwing someone out of a window is defenestration. I'm better for knowing this. Sadie is awesome.

She's particularly interested in the history of religion and how it has shaped cultures over time. It's fascinating stuff. You can't go too far into those discussions without running across creeds, and among the many, two reign supreme—the Aretha and Beyonce of summarized doctrine. These are the Apostles' Creed and the

Nicene Creed. They changed the game and their influence is everywhere.

If this were a history book, I'd tell you about the Council of Nicaea in AD 325 and the Council of Constantinople in AD 381. I'd write about how some denominations use the Apostles' Creed but remove one line, and how the Chinese Orthodox Church removes a different line from the Nicene.

Since this is not a history book, I'll just say that it's a rabbit hole worth getting lost in.[19] It's endlessly interesting, and there is so much to discover and learn. If you do get curious and dig into the history, it will only add to the experience the next time—or the first time—you find yourself in a church service where everyone stands and recites one of these creeds together.

If what I'm talking about sounds unfamiliar to you, it was to me for many years too. I'd witnessed churches using them a few times in my early music travels but didn't pay it much attention. Finally, one day, I realized what was happening. An entire room was standing up and saying, at the same time, what they believed together, an almost unthinkable experience in this era of individualism and skepticism.

Creeds are a statement of belief, *of shared belief*, which makes them, by their very nature, countercultural in our modern society.

We do not like to be told what to believe. We especially do not like to be told what we *do* believe. Yet, that's exactly what these statements do.

"I believe" they might begin, or even "We believe," and then proceed to walk through a specific list of theological positions: about the nature of God and the Trinity, about Jesus' death and resurrection, and about the future of the world and the kingdom to come.

In an age where one of the greatest social sins is to impose your beliefs on another, it's a strange feeling to join your voice with a group of people and commit to sharing a point of view. To say as one, there is no "my truth," there is only "*the* truth," and we agree that it's *this thing right here*.

While these creeds are foundational, they are not comprehensive to every detail. We can agree on the creeds and disagree on tax policy or the starting lineup of the Packers or Backstreet Boys vs. NSYNC. We can vote red or blue or green or purple. These statements are not about our opinions or perspectives, or really about us at all. They are about God—who He is, what He has done for us, and what He is doing now and will do in the future with us and for us—the ones He loves.

Online, on TV, in my own head, it's just fighting and angst everywhere. Agreeing is so unusual and so wonderful, and I find such joy in saying these creeds with my brothers and sisters. It is like aloe on a sunburn, to realize that, not only do we affirm the things that matter the most, but if they really are true, *then our agreeing on them has no bearing on their truth anyway.*

They are true because God is.

They are good because God is.

And they give us hope because of who they tell us God is.

You can easily find each of these creeds in slightly different forms online. But it's worth printing them here.

THE APOSTLES' CREED

I believe in God, the Father almighty,
creator of heaven and earth.
I believe in Jesus Christ, his only Son, our Lord,
who was conceived by the Holy Spirit,
born of the Virgin Mary,
suffered under Pontius Pilate,
was crucified, died,
and was buried;
he descended to the dead.
On the third day he rose again;
he ascended into heaven,
he is seated at the right hand of the Father,
and he will come to judge the living and the dead.
I believe in the Holy Spirit,
the holy catholic Church,
the communion of saints,
the forgiveness of sins,
the resurrection of the body,
and the life everlasting.
Amen.

THE NICENE CREED

We believe in one God,
the Father, the Almighty,
maker of heaven and earth,
of all that is, seen and unseen.

We believe in one Lord,
Jesus Christ,
the only Son of God,
eternally begotten of the Father,
God from God, Light from Light,
true God from true God
begotten, not made,
of one Being with the Father.
Through him all things
were made.
For us and for our salvation
he came down from heaven:
by the power of the Holy Spirit
he became incarnate from the
Virgin Mary,
and was made man.
For our sake he was crucified
under Pontius Pilate;
he suffered death and
was buried.

On the third day he rose again
in accordance with the Scriptures;
he ascended into heaven
and is seated at the right hand of
the Father.
He will come again in glory to
judge the living and the dead,
and his kingdom will have no
end.

We believe in the Holy Spirit,
the Lord, the giver of life,
who proceeds from the
Father and the Son.
With the Father and the Son he is
worshiped and glorified.
He has spoken through the
Prophets.

We believe in one holy catholic
and apostolic Church.
We acknowledge one baptism
for the forgiveness of sins.
We look for the resurrection
of the dead,
and the life of the world to come.
Amen.

27.

Play the Rests

QUIET TOGETHER

EVERY DECEMBER I'M HONORED TO be a part of Andrew Peterson's *Behold the Lamb of God* Christmas tour, a beautiful musical retelling of the story of Christ's arrival on earth, with a large and stellar cast of musicians. Every year, if I'm honest, I also show up feeling like my skills are not quite on par with everybody else's and I worry that this is the year they'll figure it out.

Usually this means I end up trying too hard and playing too much, filling every little hole in the music with some extra flourishes to make sure I come across as competent and professional, but really end up making extra clutter and a higher likelihood of mistakes.

Apparently, I'm not the only one.

After our first couple of shows every single year, Ben Shive, our genius musical director, has the same conversation with the band: "Okay, guys, you're all great. We just need to remember to make space for each other. Let's all try to keep to our parts, listen to each other, and play the rests." Then we all settle down, play less, have more fun, and sound way better.

One of the most important lessons you learn as a musician is that not playing is often as powerful as the notes you play.

Rests are what it's called in music when you take a break between phrases or sections. Sometimes the sections are a few bars, sometimes a few minutes. To pay attention and be present in those periods is what musicians have unofficially dubbed "playing the rests." It's something highly lauded in legendary players of many genres such as jazz, blues, classical, and folk. They are known as much for their restraint as for their ability.

If you're a singer or you play a wind instrument, those rests are time you spend catching your breath. If you're a piano player or a guitarist like me, you're not just waiting to play again, you're listening to what else is happening around you: Who else is contributing? What other melodies are hanging in the air that you can play off of or respond to? Do you need to enter more loudly or more gently? The resting is actively listening.

Some of the best shows I've ever performed are the ones where I've played the least notes but have done the most listening.

Yet it is always a challenge between ego and service, and between self-doubt and confidence. I pray more and more now as I play, asking God to guide my fingers in humility and away from selfishness and pride (and wrong notes!).

Why is playing less so hard? Why is it so hard to be quiet?

Quiet is a foreign land, not just for musicians, but for *all* of us now living in this unnatural state of constant entertainment and stimulation.

I usually have a steady stream of podcasts, Spotify, or YouTube on my AirPods. There's background music in the elevator. The home makeover twins are on the TV in the doctor's office lobby. We are almost never quiet. We don't know how to handle it.

I remember how odd it was when Alison and I were newlyweds and finally realized it was okay to just sit and be quiet in the house we now shared. We'd been talking for the last few years, sharing our stories, laughing, making memories, making plans. At first it felt a little strange to just "be" together and not be constantly doing something. But it also felt so natural and nice. Like we were settling in to something deeper.

This is yet another gift of communal time together in worship before God, that in some traditions, and historically even most traditions, we have had moments of quiet. These moments are not for listening to each other play music, but actually being quiet together, listening to our own thoughts and hearts. Listening for the heart of God.

Christians are gifted with quiet in times of confession. We have times of prayer for other people, which is intercessory prayer. We're quietly meditating on certain Scriptures and psalms.

It might be quick; it might last a while. It can be unnerving and awkward, or just plain boring. Possibly transcendent. It could be all those things at the same time.

Some of the most profound moments of my faith have happened in moments of group quiet.

YoungLife camps send kids out to sit under the stars and talk to God for twenty minutes the night before they go home. They've had an amazing week and heard all about Jesus, but need time to process it. To actually think and talk to God about it. My own life was changed this way, as were those of many of my friends.

I've been in spiritual direction groups where we've prayed together around certain Scriptures and then sat in silence to meditate on them, sometimes for a long period of time.

During one of those periods I got a business idea that radically reshaped the past few years of my career. The next time we did it, I'm pretty sure I fell asleep. I think God was giving me what I needed both times.

My own church doesn't do long periods of quiet very often, though as I've traveled, I've had some amazing experiences in other churches that do.

A few years ago, I found myself in the oldest church on the islands of Hawaii, a beautiful, open-air Catholic chapel. It could not have been more different from the Chicago airport of my first Mass experience. The building was gorgeous, the congregation was lively, and the priest engaged.

It was an early morning service, and the sunrise was streaming through the windows as a breeze blew across the pews. We sang a hymn, recited a few prayers and Scriptures, and then were led in silent meditation on a psalm for maybe the longest time I've ever experienced in a church.

My mind went through so many stages. "Oh cool, how refreshing." "Okay, this is going kind of long." "Wow, this is boring." "This seat is uncomfortable." "I should really think about that Scripture again." "That verse is profound." "Jesus loves me, and I'm overwhelmed trying to think about it."

I was sad when the time of quiet ended. I did not realize how much I needed it.

Many church services today are held in rooms labeled the "worship center," but previous generations, even here in America, would have worshiped in the "sanctuary."

Sanctuary is a word with two meanings.

The first is a holy space, devoted only to gather for worship and prayer. A place set apart for the sacred life of a community: the mundane, the mourning, and the celebration.

The second meaning was actually created by the work of

churches that used their sanctuaries for people in need of shelter, whether they were escaping an evil tyrant or the consequences of their own lawbreaking. As long as they were in that church building, they were "given sanctuary" and allowed to stay there safe, free, and unharmed.

Refugees are given sanctuary, and sanctuary cities today are a hot political topic, but the root stems from the church offering shelter to those in need . . . the most beautiful way for a noun to become a verb.

Here in the age of misinformation, personalized ads, and entertainment everywhere (what will we do if we're not entertained?!), what do we need more than sanctuary from it all? A safe place for God's people where, though we may have even brought it on ourselves, the noise and condemnation of the world is not allowed to touch us.

There, in the stillness, we can finally stop playing and trying to prove ourselves worthy. We can, if we're willing, play the rests and listen together; listen for the melodies of mercy and the harmonies of comfort that God is playing just for us.

28.

Postures

GROWING UP AS A FUNDAMENTALIST, we were told to beware of premarital sex because it could lead to dancing.[20]

The most we fundies moved in our worship services was standing to sing or pray.

It might be hard to fully imagine how shocking it was the first time I witnessed people actually dancing or lifting their hands in a church service, let alone the flag waving and running up and down the aisle that I experience when I hang out with some of my more charismatic friends.

These days, it's almost hard to comprehend my surprise. A charismatic movement is currently sweeping around the world. You can see this in the language of our worship songs or by any simple Google image search of the word "worship." What you'll see is a group of people standing up, eyes closed, hands lifted high; a sight that would have looked unfamiliar to most American Christians even fifty years ago, when hands were too busy to be raised because they were holding a hymnal.

Every week, it seems, I read a new headline in a scientific outlet that tells of the link between the body and the mind. Something happens within us when we move that connects what we think with what we feel.

I'm a guitar player, not a neuroscientist (though I find their work fascinating and love to read about it), but I recognize this pattern in my own life. When I make myself go out and take a walk, I often discover I enjoy it midway through. When I, maybe begrudgingly, get off the couch and do something to serve my wife or daughters, I find I feel more loving toward them in the process (or afterward).

The postures we take shape who we become.

This also means that, in some ways, the more we physically practice who we'd like to be, the more we will find ourselves being those people. We can practice caring for others, or exercising, or getting up on time, and eventually turn out to be somebody who does that stuff! Crazy how hard we make it sometimes, isn't it?

What postures, then, do we want to adopt before God?

We stand, we sit, we may even lift our hands and sing at the top of our lungs. Do these shape us to be people who live honorably, sit under authority, and give praise where praise is due?

I've realized there is one posture we sing about in our songs that, until I found myself in a "liturgical" tradition, I rarely if ever took on a regular position.

"Here I am to worship," the song says, "here I am to bow down."[21]

But did I?

That act of submission: of getting on my knees, bowing my head, admitting my surrender and His glory . . . it is a posture of humility. A beggar at the foot of God's door, accepting my role as one in need and not the one in charge.

And yet! Like all things in the kingdom of God, that is not the end of the story. The beggar gets not only a scrap of bread, but a blessing and an invitation to join the family. To bow before this King is also then the posture of receiving.

In liturgical traditions, Communion is served while bowing. "This is my body, broken for you. This is my blood poured for you. Take, eat, drink."

To bow before a King who would offer you Himself? It's almost too good to be true.

If the postures we take shape who we become, then let me bow here a little longer.

This is where I need to be.

29.

Symbols

HANGING IN THE MONASTERY OF Saint Catherine on Mount Sinai in Egypt is a sixth-century Byzantine icon, a startling image of Jesus. If you were to cover one side of the painting, He would be looking at you with compassion and kindness. Move your hand to the other side and Jesus would raise His eyebrow, tighten His jaw, and fix you with a stern reproach.[22]

This is meant to show the duality of Jesus: both God and man. His justice and His mercy.

Fundamentalist theology raised me under one eye, Christian radio sings of the other, yet both are true. This painting and others of that type are meant to teach hard-to-grasp themes like this.

Our former priest Thomas loved that icon and hung a copy of it in our church. It's a challenging portrait, one I've stared at for a long time, over and over. It's haunting and it asks something of you every time you give it your attention.

I have sat in many boardroom meetings about Christian music, books, and movies where I've been told by marketing executives and data specialists that Christians don't "get" symbolism, that they want their stories told straight and clear, without metaphor or ambiguity. "None of that artsy stuff, just get to the point."

I simply can't agree with this.

First, you who are reading this right now, you are not dumb. God gave you an amazing mind that can do incredible things. Just because it's easier for someone else to market simple things to you does not mean that's what *you* like most or what is best for you. Do not give them that power over you.

Second, Jesus taught almost exclusively in metaphors and symbolism. He rarely explained His parables, and when He did, much of the time, it only got more confusing. We are meant to chew on this stuff. To hammer it out; to discover.

To be handed a thousand dollars is not as rewarding as earning it. We value what we have to work for.

This icon is just one of a million thoughtful, little secrets, hidden in plain sight throughout the church's history, that the contemporary church has lost in its move toward streamlining its methods and message. There are few mysteries to uncover in a spotlight and a headset mic, as helpful as those tools can be.

For instance, I'd attended an Anglican church for a couple years before I tried to make a joke to Father Thomas: "Cool green scarf, man. I like how you match all the banners hanging around."

"I have to, dude. That's my job." That's how he talked.

When I asked what he meant he realized I had no idea what I was really asking, so he started to teach me. This is where I first learned that Anglicans, along with many other denominations (Eastern Orthodox, Lutherans, Methodists, Catholics, and some Reformed churches) follow the church calendar, laid out (for our tradition) in the *Book of Common Prayer*. Every three years we cycle through the same weekly Sunday readings, plus a two-year daily personal rotation.

That calendar is broken into different seasons, each marked by a different color, and these are what the priests wear and how the altar is decorated.

"Whoa," I said. There was so much more going on than I realized. Here I thought he just liked green.

He wore green the most, I learned, because it meant Ordinary Time, the most common color throughout the year. Green represents life, growth, and hope, and is a symbol of our continual flourishing in Christ.

Purple is the color for Advent and Lent—seasons of preparation leading up to Christmas and Easter—both times of waiting: for the birth of Christ and for His death and resurrection.

White (or gold) is for Christmas and Easter (which are both seasons, not just days!), plus other feast days and special occasions like weddings, funerals, or baptisms. This represents light, joy, and purity and celebrates Christ's birth and resurrection.

So, yeah, this definitely *was* his job, dude.

Once I knew about this little piece of symbolism in the liturgical service, I started paying attention and, like hidden Mickeys at Disney World, once you have eyes for them, you start to see these types of symbols everywhere.

People were making the sign of the cross when they prayed, invoking the Holy Trinity. They were bowing as an actual physical cross passed by during a procession that began the service. I realized that the Scripture readings weren't called readings, they were called "Lessons." *But nobody was teaching anything . . .*

Oh! Just reading Scripture is a lesson by itself . . . *Incredible.* Got it.

When they read from the Gospels, they would bring the Bible down into the middle of the sanctuary and read it from there, to signify Jesus coming down from heaven to meet us on earth. *You've got to be kidding me.*

How to Remember

The pinnacle of a liturgical service was not, like every worship service I'd ever attended, a man getting up and preaching a sermon. Here that happened in the middle (and was quite a bit shorter) and instead, the highest point of the service was each of us kneeling down and taking Communion. Every week. However long it took.

Everything from the design of the wooden crosses to the order of the service was happening for a specific reason; to hint or signify some deeper truth, so that everywhere you looked, in every motion happening around you, a silent symphony was playing its subtle song of spiritual formation.

To be very clear: Our church doesn't do it the best way, or the "right" way—just one way. But it was seeing this way that opened my eyes to the many ways that symbolism could be communicating the message of the gospel when people took the time to craft the time of worship with that level of intention.

Our small congregation in Nashville is not special. All around the world you'll find doves and fig leaves carved into houses of worship; lions and lambs in watercolor on the walls. Candles in threes and sevens, their flames being hidden like Christ in the tomb, or passed from neighbor to neighbor to celebrate His birth and rising again. Messages being sung by choirs and shouted by preachers or hidden in architecture and whispered in ritual.

Whether we realize it or not, these intentional pictures are invitations to experience the sights, sounds, smells, tastes, and touch of the good news of Jesus. These symbols teach us, shape us, and stay with us, in ways that words cannot.

GARDEN

in the beginning
God was walking through the garden
in the cool of the day

Adam walked with God
Eve knew Him and was known by Him

but after the fruit

the beasts grew wild
the labor painful

Judas led a mob
to a garden
in the dead of night

Christ the Messiah
walked with His captors
toward the hill where He was to die

but here,

until that garden
where the beasts walk freely
with the sons of man

we have only this:

an invitation

to walk
in the day
or the night
with God

30.

The Quiet Hours

THIS MORNING I WAS SUPPOSED to meet a friend out at Radnor Lake. I was looking forward to hanging with him, but when he had to cancel, a big part of me was relieved. As much as I enjoy time with my friend, I was more excited to go walking by myself.

I knew I needed it.

For a long time, I had thought this feeling was selfish. You're not supposed to prioritize your own needs over those of others, I'd been told (or maybe I'd just assumed). To be clear, I believe very strongly that we *are* meant to serve others more than ourselves.

But I also know that if my leg is broken and I have pneumonia, I can serve people better if I first go to the doctor, get some medicine, and have my leg taken care of.

When you read the Bible a tiny little bit at a time, it might be easy to miss it, but if you ever sit down and read a big section of any of the Gospels in one sitting, you'll find this fact glaring:

Jesus is disappearing all the time.

This holy ghosting is not supernatural or miraculous, but a counterculcural, ambition-busting, commonsense prioritizing of mental, emotional, and spiritual health.

Following a day of miracles in Capernaum, early in His ministry, and before a day of monumental decisions like choosing the apostles, Jesus went off to a solitary place. After He famously feeds the five thousand, He retreats to a mountainside to pray, before finally reappearing to His friends who are in their boat by walking to them across the water. (See Mark 1:35–37; Luke 6:12–13; Matt. 14:19–25.)

> *Yet the news about him spread all the more, so that crowds of people came to hear him and to be healed of their sicknesses. But Jesus often withdrew to lonely places and prayed. (Luke 5:15–16)*

On the night of His betrayal and arrest, Jesus went to a garden called Gethsemane, leaving His disciples and walking farther up into the hills to be alone. What followed were some of the barest and most honest words of sorrow and surrender heard in the Bible, spoken by the Son of God Himself, recorded in Matthew 26:36–44.

If Jesus is constantly needing to sneak away to find quiet places to be alone and pray, then, friends—maybe we need this too.

My parents have had regular quiet times in the morning, in the same chairs, at the same time, every day for years and years. For most of my life, I've felt guilty that I've not been able to be steady and consistent like they are.

They've also always had jobs where they went to the same place, every day at the same time, and woke up in the same city. Their days are consistent. Things that have rarely been true in my life. I have had to make different rhythms.

When I'm home, I have Radnor Lake, or a walk around my own neighborhood. I am given quiet moments in the living room once everyone is finally asleep and I can use that time to "go off to the hills and pray" by simply turning off all the screens and sitting in the stillness.

When I'm traveling, there is usually a park, or at least a sidewalk, somewhere nearby. It might take a bit of creativity or planning, but it has almost always been possible to find a few minutes alone to think, talk, and listen to God.

Now that I'm here, can I find the courage to tell God what's really going on? About my marriage, my kids, and my career? Can I talk to Him about money and sex and the burden of my unmet expectations and desires?

"Father, take this cup from me," cried Jesus on the hillside, the night He was betrayed.

If I can't talk about this stuff here, then there really is no other safe place in my life to share it.

Those emotions will come out, of course, as stupid decisions, or punches and jabs at people I care about, all because I have not gone off to that quiet place and faced them honestly, alone with God.

We can talk to God there, yes, but we can also listen. That's the harder part, isn't it? To sit in silence and wait . . .

To "be still, and know" that He is God, as we're invited in Psalm 46:10.

I can't tell you what God might have for you, of course. He can literally do and say anything, but often He does or says nothing, or at least nothing we notice in the moment. We are listening for the voice of mystery, after all, and mystery is often what we hear.

Other times, we listen and find that, well, sitting on a rock felt like sitting on a rock, and that was about it.

Sometimes we listen and we don't hear an audible voice from God, because we get distracted by a feeling that we now kind of understand what we ought to do about that situation we'd been praying over, and we have an idea that might solve our problem. Maybe we realize we have a few calls we need to make, or a word going through our mind that we just can't shake.

We might listen and hear nothing, but see the birds fly across the river and the deer leading their young up a hill. Slowly, a peace seems to surround us on the breath of the wind, and we can't help but whisper: "Is that You?"

And then there are those moments, so rare we almost can't believe they're possible—until suddenly they're the only thing that is—we listen and we might experience what the Puritans call "God's kisses";[23] a moment when God seems to almost physically wrap us up in His love, we sense it so deeply and completely. Whatever name humans have tried to put on this experience, if we've ever felt it, we know.

Like a kiss, it does not last forever, nor could it be our entire relationship, yet it is a staggering overwhelming of the senses; one that lasts in our memory for years, oftentimes leaving us with a distinct before and after.

The Father may not take the cup of suffering away, but we know, in a more tangible way, that we are not alone and that the sun will surely rise over even the darkest night.

I think I might just be starting to understand why Jesus keeps sneaking away. Whatever I might hear, whatever I need to say, none of that conversation happens unless I "withdraw to lonely places and pray."

As I grow older, I find myself a little less drawn into the spectacle of Jesus' miracles, and a little more curious about where Jesus might be headed afterward.

In every story now, I'm keeping my eye on Him. He's right in the middle of things, but at any minute, I know, He might just sneak out of the frame and go walking up that hill, disappearing between the trees...

31.

Guided Prayer

GOD HAS FILLED US WITH desire and longing and purpose and intent. One of those deepest desires is an intimate and trustworthy connection with Him.

We know, too, that this connection is called prayer, yet when we're disconnected from our own hearts and lives, prayer feels like making paper boats, placing them in a river, and watching them drift away, hoping they'll somehow make it all the way to the ocean.

If we were sick, we would call a doctor. If we're lost, which it sounds like we might be, then it might be time to look for a guide.

Thankfully, and mercifully, there are guides who have gone before us down this river to the ocean of God's presence (and thankfully and mercifully, if the ocean is God's presence, that means the rivers and streams are too).

Jesus Himself was the first guide, teaching us to pray in His sermon on the mountainside. Over the centuries that have followed, others have developed tools helpful for shaping daily rhythms, for Scripture meditations, and even for helping pull us out of the distraction of impulse/response living and drawing us back toward Christ.

The contemporary American church has largely abandoned these practices, but finding and starting to use them in my own life over the past few years has been, for me, life-changing. I still slip into the fog of busyness and worry but knowing how to follow the guides of prayer practices like these offers me a way back to God and to myself.

The first of these practices I learned about is called *Lectio Divina*.

I was at a retreat at a lodge in British Columbia years ago, sitting on a cliff above the Princess Louisa inlet, where a man named Al, a counselor and friend of many of us there, began telling us about an ancient monastic practice whose roots could be traced back to the third century—to guys with names like Ambrose of Milan and Augustine of Hippo.[24] He then led us in the exercise, and I was shaken. In my thirty years as a Christian, I'd never experienced prayer so intensely, so personal, or so intentionally.

Lectio Divina is based around the idea that the Scripture is indeed the living Word of God, to be entered into rather than simply studied. By praying *with* the words of Scripture, we can hear God's voice in deeper, more resonant ways. Over the centuries it has formalized into a four-movement process.[25]

> **Read** (*Lectio*): A leader will read a passage of Scripture slowly. Take it in. What is happening? Who are the characters? The setting? The words being used?
>
> **Meditate** (*Meditatio*): We reflect on the text and what it means. How does this text relate to our lives? Our situations or those we care about? Our wounds or those we have wounded?

Pray (*Oratio*): In prayer, we respond to God. What must we confess? What do we need? What do we desire? Where do we hurt? What do we long for?

Contemplate (*Contemplatio*): In silence, we rest in the presence of God.

Often, in a group setting, the first three steps will be repeated before resting for a time. A following exercise might include sharing what word or phrase of the passage "shimmers." What has God highlighted specifically in the passage, which may be very different from person to person, and what significance did that carry?

It's been astonishing, in my experience, to see the different things God is communicating to His children through the same short passage.

The Liturgy of the Hours is an ancient form of daily liturgical prayer I have found to be a particularly beautiful and helpful tool in my own life, and is what I often use, personally.

Historically, there were seven "hours" or periods to pause for prayer and worship throughout the day, each set roughly three hours apart.[26] Over the years, particularly across traditions, some of the names and schedules have shifted or consolidated, yet the core idea has remained. Today, many believers practice condensed versions of the liturgies,[27] centering around these four "hours":

Lauds: praise at dawn to greet the day

Midday: a pause at noon to reorient and refocus

Vespers: evening prayer at the setting of the sun

Compline: the final prayer at night, right before you go to sleep

How to Remember

At each of these times, you pause your day for a few moments and follow as the liturgies lead you through prayers of praise, prayers for mercy and protection, and prayers for others, as well as readings from the Psalms, the day's Scriptures, the Nicene Creed, and a time for confession.

Like all liturgical offerings, the readings can seem very similar, yet on closer inspection are intuitively unique. Mornings tend to focus on light, resurrection, and hope, vespers on confession and intercession, while evening focuses more on thanksgiving and rest. Like a liturgical church service, what can seem rote at first, over time becomes powerful and deeply formative.

Don't be put off by the word "hours," either. These liturgies typically take me ten to twenty minutes, depending on that day's readings.

You can find *The Liturgy of the Hours* in many forms: books, websites, apps, or subscriptions emailed to you.[28] Each may differ slightly in the particulars offered, but all will follow this general outline.

Finally, a form of personal prayer often used at the end of the day, though it can be used throughout, is called the Examen. My Catholic friends know this well and pray a form of it daily. It was created by Ignatius of Loyola in his 1524 book *Spiritual Exercises*. The Examen is a prayerful reflection on the happenings of the day. Through it we see both our actions and motivations and God's presence and direction more clearly.

Though many people and traditions have created variations over the years, they all follow some form of the original five points.[29]

1. *Give thanks to God for the good I have received.*

2. *Ask for grace to know my sins and rid myself of them.*

3. *Ask for an account of my soul—my thoughts, words, and actions—through the day until now.*

4. *Ask forgiveness from God for my faults.*

5. *Resolve, with God's grace, to amend them.*

These are just three of the primary guides for prayer that Christians have developed over the centuries.

These are like paths in national parks. No one owns them (or maybe we all do) and some people are working to keep the paths clean and clear for the rest of us. If one of these is helpful for you, that's wonderful. If it's another form out there, fantastic. We're all looking to get to the same place—closer to the heart of Christ.

32.

Sacred Spaces

FOR A FEW YEARS, I showed up very early on Sundays to set up chairs in a nightclub, often just an hour or two after the punk shows had packed out and gone home, so that we could have church there that morning. A few years later we did the same thing in an elementary school cafeteria. Basically, as long as you had a vomit mop handy, it was a place we could have church. Without a doubt, before and behind every eight-hundred-year-old cathedral is the story of hundreds of years of folding chairs and fundraising. It has to start somewhere.

What a testament—how the church continues to grow anywhere and everywhere, on the rockiest cliff and the thinnest of soil.

I think God takes great delight in *our* delight of new things and old things. (The cathedrals that are so old to us were once the height of innovation and progress, after all.) I imagine He enjoys the thrill we get from architecture and creativity and responsible budgeting and lavish gift-giving, and all the ways human beings use the gifts He has given them to joyfully serve others and honor Him in return.

My daughter Ella spent a couple of semesters studying in Madrid, and many weekends she and her roommates would grab their backpacks, hop on trains and planes, and travel across Europe. She's the kind of person who sees life as a challenge to pack as much in as she can, while carrying as little in her bag as possible. She was made for this type of trip.

One Nashville morning, we woke up to text messages from Ella that the night before she just happened to be in Paris, France, walking near the Cathedral of Notre Dame the first time the bells rang after its reconstruction from the fire of 2019.

Notre Dame is so old it was actually built before the Aztec empire. It is the absolute heart of the city. Wild fact: Every building or street in Paris is numbered by its distance to the cathedral.

"It was amazing," she told me. "There were thousands of people on the streets, and as soon as the bells rang, it instantly got silent. Everyone just stood there and listened. We all started tearing up. It was the most beautiful thing, Dad. I will never forget it."

Just imagine her experience had she gotten inside the building. All this was still a quarter of a mile away.

If you've ever set foot inside a cathedral, you know immediately that it is unlike any other kind of building. The sheer immensity and grandeur take your breath away. You don't know where to look. There are paintings everywhere; archways, stained glass, rooms and hallways, statues . . . it overwhelms the senses.

There's symbolism wherever you look. Simply standing in the room is a master class in theology.

Cathedral sanctuaries are usually built in cruciform, where their floor plan takes the shape of the cross. The horizontal arms represent humanity, while the longer vertical axis reflects divine interaction. Typically, there are stained glass windows depicting stories from the Bible and church history, so simply walking around is a journey through a "visual Bible." The east-facing altar, symbolizing Jesus rising with the sun every morning, is elevated at the center of the room, beneath a large cross, so that the focus of the room is on the cross and the altar. Height and light interplay inside to evoke awe and reverence, while the spire outside calls out like a beacon, visible from afar, as a reminder to all around of the steadfast presence of God.

I've been in the country's biggest megachurches. They don't hold a candle to a cathedral. There is no modern American equivalent.

A cathedral is a skyscraper, though. It's meant for a city. It's a huge building for a huge population. You're not going to find something that big and grand in a village of five hundred people. But if you drive by an old town in the northeastern American countryside, you will quickly see one building that stands out among and above all the others. It looks different because it is different. When you watch an old Western, in those towns there might only be six buildings, but one of them looks different because it is different.

Old church buildings, and the spaces within them, are fundamentally other—just like the God they are there to honor.

Sometimes after I drop my daughter off at school, I go running, and I often park my car at the Episcopal church near her school. Often they leave the sanctuary open so people can go in and pray. I don't attend there, but I'll go in sometimes and take a few minutes. It's a beautiful, quiet room with a big arched ceiling. It probably seats five or six hundred people, and there are no screens, so when you walk in all your attention is immediately drawn to the cross on the back wall. It is very clear what this room is about. There's an inherent sense of reverence.

When I step into a room with stadium seating, great lighting, and a video wall, I know that our show is going to look and sound great that night, but I don't feel the same reverence. Nothing about that room slows me down or offers invitation. It may be an excellent place for people to worship, but it is no sanctuary.

I don't for a minute think that my church or your church in this moment of this culture needs to build a Gothic cathedral. Again, in their time those were groundbreaking works of architecture with forward-thinking technology, pairing available materials with their contemporary art.

Imagine the legacy, though, if churches across the country (that are fortunate enough to invest in their own spaces) built not primarily for efficiency, but with larger goals of beauty, symbolism, and sanctuary. What if the map was dotted with monuments around the nation, set apart to honor a God who is altogether different and holy?

What if people driving around the streets of our city could learn about God, not from cheesy signs on a billboard out front, but from the way the very buildings themselves were shaped and formed?

Maybe some churches have the resources to build a worship center *and* a sanctuary or a chapel, so they can do the light show and the video wall but also offer that sacred space.

I know it's far easier to offer critique when I'm not the one raising the money or drafting the budgets, and please don't think I'm judging anyone or telling people what to do. I guess what I'm really doing here is asking—pleading—because I feel so deeply a need that I think we don't even realize we're all desperate for—holy refuge and inspiring beauty.

And of course, there are many who have answered this call in the most unique and incredible ways here in America, like the

Chapel of the Holy Cross in Sedona, Arizona, the Air Force Chapel in Colorado Springs, and the St. Louis Basilica.

Really, before we began to mass-produce worship services and streamline our buildings toward that end, the fabric of America's landscape was stitched with farmland country steeples, quietly beautiful chapels, and city-facing downtown churches.

Just as God speaks to us through music, film, food, and literature, God has also through the ages spoken to our cities, neighborhoods, families, and worshipers through the minds and hearts of His architects, builders, and designers. If only more communities could be served by sacred rooms like these again—rooms that inspire reverence, awe, and the awareness of holiness!

Rather than trying to compete with the world's never-ending thirst for entertainment and optimization, these buildings have joined in the tradition of wonderfully created sanctuary spaces, rich with symbolism and beauty, rest and retreat.

33.

Coloring on the Wall

WHEN OUR CHURCH MOVED INTO its current building, our priest, Thomas, was sad that there was not a real cross at the head of the sanctuary, just an old stained glass window that kind of suggested the shape of one in an ugly, flowery sort of fashion.[30] The problem was, where do you get a twelve-foot-tall cross, anyway? They don't sell those on Amazon.

My friend Mark is a music publisher, but we all know him as the man with a million hobbies. He keeps bees, rides motorcycles, and makes his own wine. He's also a welder and woodworker.

We tragically lost Thomas in a car accident a few years ago, and the church dearly misses him. Whenever we talk about Thomas, we remember his fierce loyalty to his friends and family, his radical love of the gospel, and his . . . opinions. He had many, and we all knew them. Twenty or thirty years from now he would have been the most hilarious cranky old man with a heart of gold. He already was in his forties.

It didn't take long, then, for Mark to figure out just how much Thomas hated that wispy, frilly, stained glass cross, and how he wanted a "real, Anglican cross" up there. So Mark decided to make one. It took eight months of nights and weekends in a friend's garage (because a twelve-foot cross was not going to fit in his) and finally it was done.

It's been hanging there now for fifteen years or so. It's watched over countless Communions, hymns, and sermons; dozens of weddings, funerals, baptisms, and cute little kids in Christmas pageants. I forget about it for a while and then every now and then it catches my eye and I remember, "oh yeah, Mark built that!"

Every Sunday morning there are two big vases of flowers on either side of the cross too. Different families take turns signing up to fill them, and someone else comes early to arrange it all and make them look beautiful.

Debbie is a painter, and she has a beautiful piece representing the Trinity that hangs in the entryway to the sanctuary there, between the parking lot doors and the stairs to the basement. For years she also organized different art pieces made by the church family to hang between the windows of the sanctuary to represent the fourteen Stations of the Cross, an ancient miniature pilgrimage Christians use to follow, and enter into, the suffering and events of the day of Jesus' death.

Jeff was our sexton for years—taking care of the building and the grounds, until he had to step back to spend more time taking care of his dad. He still mows the lawn each week, though, and the place never fails to look beautiful and welcoming.

It's a church home because people are making it their own, and you feel that as you walk around, whether you know these stories or not.

My friend Russ, the "HANG IN THERE" guy, is a pastor who

loves art history. His church meets in a business park, not the most inspiring bit of real estate, but he has decorated the walls with art so that it feels like a museum. Everywhere you look there's a Monet or a Rembrandt, with a little card next to it telling the story of the painting, and some way that it relates to the gospel. It's very beautiful and it's very Russ.

We might worry that things like people's art or flowers might seem old-fashioned or cluttered. Too personal. Not professional or excellent. We might worry that asking folks to do things like painting a picture, bringing their toolbox, or using whatever their gifts are might be an imposition, a bother. Too much of a wild card.

To that I would ask: Do you feel at home in a hotel? Welcomed in a conference center?

We are a people desperate for belonging. Especially in an age of such complete disconnection, we're starved for authenticity. When our country is so franchised to death you can find the bathroom in a Target in a new city with your eyes closed, places that feel "human" are becoming increasingly rare.

Not only do we need places that look and feel like people live there, *we* need to live there. We need to be involved. We need to refill the toilet paper and know where the folding chairs go and build the giant cross. We need to bring our smoker for the potluck and teach finger-knitting to the tweens. We need to walk in and see our own stories in the hallway. It's our gifts together that make this place what it is.

We need to feel ownership. If something is out of place, I know that I can put it back, because I go here and I know where it belongs. I can clean up a mess and take out the trash.

There was a season where our family didn't have a church home. We visited here for a few weeks and there for a few weeks.

We saw friends at each place and that was fun, and we'd get in the car and review the service like it was a movie. "I liked the music, but the sermon was too long." We were consumers.

When we live somewhere, it's different. We invest ourselves: our time, our thoughts, our energy, into that place and that community. We're not just going to try some other place next week.

If you want to belong, go in and ask how you can help. Look around for what might need to be done.

If it's your place and you want people to stay, invite them in and offer them something to do. If somebody wants to try something that might seem a little messy or a little unprofessional, well, keep an eye on it, but maybe let them give it a shot.

And if they end up coloring on the wall—well, my kids did that too, when they felt safe at home.

34.

Generations

FOR ALL THE SCANDAL AND corruption and everything else that has plagued the American church, there have been countless dedicated servants pouring their heart and soul into serving the church to the absolute best of their abilities. They have come in early and stayed late, filled in gaps from their own pocketbooks, and gone every extra mile imaginable.

What if (and it hurts to even ask), but what if we've been given the wrong map, and some of that work has been to drive us farther and farther in the wrong direction, with the best of intentions?

When it comes to how we treat intergenerationality, the contemporary church, we are now learning, may have inadvertently done that.

You see, new research is showing that young adults who have grown up with even a few solid relationships with people of different ages within the church are much more likely to stay in the church the rest of their lives than their disconnected peers.[31]

Yet what have we done when a family walks up to the church building for the past fifty years?

"Hello! Welcome to *Random Church*, we're so glad you're here! Four-year-olds go with the fours and fives! Seven-year-olds go with the Junior Rangers! You're twelve? You can come here with the pre-teens! And high schoolers, we've got a whole different building just for you! You never have to see or be seen by the rest of the church at all! Parents, you can pick your kids up for lunch at 12:30!"

We have the college class, the young singles, the young marrieds, the young parents, the older parents, the boomers, the silver saints. We've got a program for everyone, because we're trying to reach everyone. It's a noble cause. But if "a cord of three strands is not quickly broken" as Ecclesiastes 4:12 tells us, have we inadvertently loosened those cords and threads, and could that be part of why the ropes and nets that have historically held the church together started to fray?

Statistics show that the share of Americans who claim no religious affiliation between 1973 and now rose from 5 percent to 29 percent.[32] That's a quarter of the country in fifty years! Clearly, there are hundreds of factors contributing to this decline of belief, and also there are many different ways God will draw people back to Him.

Still, I can't help but wonder if the separation and isolation of the church by age has contributed to people feeling disconnected and more likely to wander away, and if rebuilding those relationships might be a primary means of healthy and holistic regrowth.

I'd love for you to think I became aware of this through my own keen observation of Samuel and Eli's relationship in the Old Testament—the original intergenerational friendship model in the Bible. But no, my inspiration came from a luncheon at

Belmont University, where someone spoke about this topic. I found it fascinating. So fascinating, in fact, that I kept asking questions of the team hosting the event until, eventually, they invited me to join them—becoming creative director on a songwriting project there, focused on fostering intergenerational worship.

In Every Generation is tasked with creating songs, resources, and research to help churches reunite generations in worship, both in the congregation and among those leading them. To do that first part, creating songs, we've decided to host large writing camps where we gather twenty or thirty different songwriters and work to generate new music, lyrics, or both.

Our thinking was to model intergenerational friendship for churches by first working to build friendships between generations ourselves in the writing of these songs. So we invited writers from as young as seventeen all the way up to seventy-eight to come join us.

Usually, when I host writing camps like this, we write for about three hours in the morning, then take a break to eat lunch and share what we've written, then split into different groups for the afternoon, before gathering one more time to again share what was created in that second session. In between, I tend to walk around, checking on groups, and letting them know "Hey! Thirty minutes 'til lunch!"

I will never forget during the first session of our first camp, when I went to check on one group, and behind the door were three people: Layne, a twenty-one-year-old college student; Sarah, a woman in her early thirties; and Jeff, an accordion player in his mid-seventies. They had finished writing their song, and during the writing had started to share their stories with one another and realized how much they had in common. By the time I butted in, they were sitting there in tears, praying for one another. "That was a holy moment," Sarah told me later. "They are my friends for life."

If we never released any of this music, it was already worth it, just for that.

But the song was also fantastic, so they got to record it together, and played it together in a few concerts, working side by side. They'll hopefully make memories together, get on each other's nerves, have to work through it, and choose to care for one another.

You know... friendship.

Looking back, I see that same kind of friendship was a part of my story in high school. The relational ministry model of YoungLife is set up to work this way, preferring one-on-one relationships with kids and older people in the community as the primary method of discipleship. I had a few people who really loved me and invested in me, both in YoungLife and in my church, and I see now how grounding that was.

They didn't just say encouraging things to me, either. They gave me stuff to do. Responsibility. I wasn't a very good guitar player, by any standard, but they knew I loved it, so they would have me play at church and at YoungLife club. I had to be at rehearsal, I had to know the songs, I had to practice, I had to be on time. They would let me borrow guitars or amps or whatever else that I didn't have (or know how to use) and their trust gave me something to live up to.

Sometimes, I fear, our churches' desires to be excellent don't create space for this kind of mentorship or growth. I wonder if a few missed notes or rushed fills might be worth it now and then, to welcome some younger folks to the team. Not just musically, either, but in any aspect of the life of the church, from childcare and teaching, to groundskeeping and administration, to transportation and graphic design. Opportunities to serve are opportunities to mentor, give dignity, and befriend.

The good news is that the unintended consequences of separation by age can be undone, and it won't take the span of a generation to do it.

Imagine this: A family walks up to *Random Church* and is greeted by a college student and a seventy-five-year-old at the front door, who welcome them and direct them to children's church drop-off, where members of the youth group and some of the parents and grandparents of the congregation are working together to play with kids and teach some simple lessons. (The kids *love* that the super cool high schoolers want to hang out with them, and there seems to be a special bond between the teens and the senior citizens as they wrangle the kiddos.)

Upstairs, more college kids are running sound and PowerPoint, while other teenagers are starting to play in the band, alongside a forty-five-year-old dentist/guitar player who has been giving them lessons. He has been excited for the opportunity to hang out with this younger crew, and to help them process their thoughts about college and dating and what's coming next in life. Plus they've turned him on to so much great new music.

Friendships between generations, walking side by side. Groups that are often overlooked, seeing each other by serving together. The elders mentoring the youth, and the youth valuing the elders, and flourishing happening every step in between. Mutual affection and mutual respect.

In our aching world of demographics, division, and demonization, intergenerational friendships are radical and redemptive. These are Jesus-style friendships. In His economy, small, faithful moments of generosity can change the course of many histories.

The church is like a waterfall, a constantly replenishing stream of people, never to be repeated, all shimmering and dancing in the reflected light of God's glory. Old and young. Wisdom and vigor. Let's not waste the chance God has given us of being with *these* people *right now*.

I'm reminded of what Sarah said after that first writing camp. Truly, each moment we're alive is a holy moment, and you never know who God might give you as a "friend for life."

35.

Others

TO BE PART OF A church community sometimes means being around people you love, and sometimes it means loving people you might not otherwise be around.

Belonging to a body of believers inevitably brings us into orbit with people of different generations, occupations, ethnic backgrounds, musical tastes, and political opinions.

Will we agree with everyone about everything? *Never.*

Will we have conflict? *Of course.*

Is that by design? *Probably.*

That's how God tends to do things, isn't it?

If you walk into your church and look around to see that everyone in sight looks like you, thinks like you, and has a similar story as you then you (A) have a brand-new baby church and no drama has happened yet, (B) you don't know the people in your church very well, or (C) you are in a cult and you need to leave right now.

One of the ways of Jesus, it seems, looks like setting down our preferences—the things we like and would naturally do—and picking up intention, choosing to prefer someone or something else, for a greater good.

Paul tells us in Philippians 2:

> *Do nothing out of selfish ambition or vain conceit. Rather, in humility value others above yourselves, not looking to your own interests but each of you to the interests of the others. In your relationships with one another, have the same mindset as Christ Jesus: Who, being in very nature God, did not consider equality with God something to be used to his own advantage; rather, he made himself nothing by taking the very nature of a servant. (vv. 3–6)*

I am so grateful that people have looked to my interests over their own and valued me above themselves. I know it has not always been easy.

I have been loved when I've not been lovable; when I've been clingy or bitter or trying too hard to be cool. I'm amazed and thankful that people have reached across economic or cultural divides to make me feel welcome (and yes, I realize I say that as someone who is more often in the majority than the minority, and so it is all the more humbling when I think of just how much people have lived out Philippians 2 in my most oblivious, obnoxious, privileged, white American presence).

That's the thing, the church is not a country club. We're not members paying dues to keep the putting greens manicured and the riffraff outside the gates. All are welcome here, even you and me, and that will get messy.

It's almost a given in the Gospels: If the religious leaders were on a tear and wanting to know where Jesus was, you just know He was with the people they would have deemed unclean and unworthy: the prostitutes, the addicts, and the people who'd been given too many chances and couldn't seem to stop screwing up. He was hanging with tax collectors who sold out their own people, Gentiles who oppressed them, and Samaritans who weren't as good as them. He gave time to children and lepers and the common, uneducated, working-class fishermen, shepherds, and laborers; people who could hold no power and could do nothing for Jesus or the Pharisee leaders.

He crossed every social, racial, gender, economic, and political line in the sand to be with people.

To be like Jesus, which is what we always say we want to do, means to step out past our comfortability and get to know people who aren't like us. I write this as much, if not more, to challenge myself than I do for you reading it.

This is not about charity or supporting a program, though those are great things. This is for every one of us; every color, language, and income bracket.

Within the body of Christ, we are never reaching *down* or *up*, but only *across*, to one another.

36.

Grieving

OUR PASTOR THOMAS WAS KILLED in a car crash three years ago along with his eldest child, as they were on a trip out west together on the first day of his sabbatical. He had just celebrated his fiftieth birthday.

Looking back, he had surprisingly prepared us for this. The week before he died, Father Thomas sent out an email to the church, telling us about where he and his wife, Laura, would be traveling over the next month, and who would be doing what at the church in his absence.

They had planned to walk the Camino de Santiago, a famous pilgrimage in Spain that ends at a gravesite believed by legend to be that of the apostle James. We all sensed his excitement for this trip by how often it would come up in his sermon illustrations the months before.

Thomas let us know that Father Kenny, our long-time associate rector (or pastor), would assume his duties while he was gone, while a few other people would handle some other responsibilities.

"In case something major happens, we've got the vestry (a council of lay leaders who govern a local congregation) and the bishop and all sorts of other people who can step up.

"That's the great thing about the church," he wrote a few days before he died. "None of us is that important."

What he meant, of course, was that the church could keep going without him—and it has. It's thriving and growing. He was right about that. Thomas was wrong about one thing, though.

He was important.

To us.

He would often slip little nuggets like this into his sermons. As eerie and prescient as that email was, we weren't shocked by his language. He would regularly say things like this (and I'm paraphrasing here):

"These days, when many people die, instead of funerals they will have a Celebration of Life, and I understand the impulse. But when I die, please don't celebrate. I want a funeral. I want you to be sad. I would hope that the people who love me are sad that I'm gone, that they would grieve, but not as those who have no hope! Because, my friends, you and I have hope in the resurrection of Jesus."

We live in a culture that does not deal well with grief because it is so terribly uncomfortable with the idea of death. We idealize movie stars who seem to be young forever, and we use plastic surgery and weight-loss drugs ("Guilty, your honor") ourselves to try to do the same.

As Christians, we recognize that death is terrible because it is, at its very core, unnatural. The world that God created and called "good" was overflowing with life and peace. Sin took creation by the spine and broke it over its knee. Death is the opposite of nature, as nature was intended. It is right that we would hate it and mourn it. That's what those emotions are for.

And yet . . . we have this stubborn hope, this light in the distance, in the depths and confusion of the deepest darkness. For we know that the Son of God humbled Himself and stepped into that death with us and for us, so that we might follow Him through it and out the other side, healed and whole, like never before.

It is a glorious hope. One that we sadly need to cling to over and over and over if we are going to become the people we are called to be.

"Andrew, what does grief and death have to do with calling?" you're asking.

Well, I'm glad you asked.

We are called to live like Christ: humbling ourselves and valuing others over our own lives. To love and serve people by knowing them and letting ourselves be known by them.

Opening ourselves to relationships with others, particularly to relationships diverse in age, means we will spend more time at funerals.

It's not a fun fact, but it's true.

Father Thomas planted our church twenty years ago with a handful of couples, most of whom were in their sixties or older. By the year or two before his death he had buried a great number of the founders of the church, and it weighed heavy on him. He talked about it more and more often. "I love you all and I'm glad that you're here, but I miss them, and for me, this place is not the same."

That might sound harsh, but I understood it. I think most of us did. Haven't we all loved people and lost them? Often we stuff those feelings down and try to keep them to ourselves. Thomas grieved publicly, and what we could have, and ordinarily would have, found offensive, instead just had us nodding in agreement.

"We get it, Thomas. We miss people too. Our places are not the same, either."

Again, he was somehow preparing us ahead of time to grieve. This is something that Jesus did, too, with His disciples.

> "Very truly I tell you, you will weep and mourn while the world rejoices. You will grieve, but your grief will turn to joy. A woman giving birth to a child has pain because her time has come; but when her baby is born she forgets the anguish because of her joy that a child is born into the world. So with you: Now is your time of grief, but I will see you again and you will rejoice, and no one will take away your joy." (John 16:20–22)

Three years later we still talk about Thomas often. We pray for his family left behind. We laugh at his "ornate" sense of humor and tell stories of the quiet ways he cared about people.

And we move on. We have a new priest, Father Andrew, who's wonderful (and weirdly, younger than me), and sweet Father Kenny, who has been here the whole time, shepherding us through those first few years with unimaginable wisdom and quiet strength.

Mark's big cross still hangs in the sanctuary, but we're about to repaint and change some of the colors on the walls. There are things happening Thomas would love and things he might not. And that's okay.

One of the gifts of grieving is the freedom you are given on the other side. Acknowledging your sadness and being honest about the pain before God is a path to healing—and I think it's the only path—even though we might carry the scars with us.

"Blessed are those who mourn, for they will be comforted," Jesus said in His sermon on the mountain (Matt. 5:4).

In John 11, Jesus, the Son of God, hears the news that His friend Lazarus has died. A few hours later, He will raise him from the dead, a foreshadowing of His own resurrection. Even still, knowing what He Himself is about to do, Jesus' immediate reaction of humanity and grief gives us the shortest verse in the English Bible:

"Jesus wept."

37.

Walking

IT'S ANOTHER MORNING AND I'M back out at Radnor Lake. I find it's a lot easier to focus out here.

You have different conversations when you're walking, side by side, without the distractions of a hip coffee shop or the constant buzzing of your phone. Plus, it's cheaper and good for my waistline.

Sometimes, I run into other friends on the trails, which is fun. Well, except for the time I was so lost in thought, without my inhaler on a steep hill, that I literally walked right into Sandra, and then couldn't catch my breath to apologize.

That was embarrassing.

I mostly love to walk alone, but it's great to be with old friends too. Catching up; going deep.

There's also a sweetness in welcoming new friends to town or walking with young songwriters trying to figure out how to make this whole thing work. I walk with older songwriters too, like my friend Buddy, who doesn't seem to mind as I pester him with questions, since I'm still trying to figure out how to make this whole thing work myself.

I've gotten caught in freezing rain and been drenched in sweat. I've turned an ankle and gotten some blisters.

Not one time have I been sad I spent time in the woods.

I know the trails are man-made, and as much as I love the idea of adventuring out here completely on my own and finding my own way, the truth is, I would be absolutely lost and likely injured pretty quickly.

No, the trails are a gift. They take me to the most beautiful places in the park, and they keep me from the most dangerous spots, as long as I stay on them.

When I first started coming out here, I realized I was frustrated that I wasn't really seeing much of the nature I'd come out to actually enjoy. To stay on the trail, I had to have my vision locked on the ground, rarely able to lift my eyes. Now I understand, the more I walk these paths, the less I need to worry about that focus. I know these trails by instinct. My feet know where to go, so I'm more free to look around and take in the beauty that surrounds me.

The same has been true of these songs, prayers, and practices I've spent the past twenty-five years discovering. My feet have learned some of those trails, and I can enjoy them now in ways I could not at first. I can worry less about which songs my heart needs to hear or how to use certain forms of prayer and instead enter more deeply into the practice of the presence of God that their repeated use has taught me.

I'm thankful, too, for the church I grew up in, and every church that has ever used my songs or invited me in to share them in person. While it's not possible to agree with every piece of every church's (or every friend's) theology, I hope that I am trusting more and more in only the Father, the Spirit, and the risen Jesus, and am becoming more and more gracious about everything else.

After all the people I've met and the ways I've seen God work in them and through them, I deeply believe that most of us are trying the best we can to faithfully follow Jesus and serve and love others. Even though we mess it up again and again and again.

The capitalist consumer mindset of American empire has been so pervasive and instinctive for those of us raised in it that it can be hard to imagine there might be more beyond it until someone shows it to us. If you, like me, have felt that longing for deeper connection with God than what a product on a shelf can offer you, I hope this book has pointed you toward some of the paths that have been carved in the woods by generations before us.

You might even start to see that there are more of us walking these paths than you realize.

And if you want to join me, you'll know where to find me.

I'll be back here tomorrow.

38.

Trees

REMEMBER THOSE TREES IN MY backyard? The ones that had to come down because they were so diseased and hollow?

A year later, I've got fifteen new trees, of all different types, fresh in the ground. They're soaking up the rain, putting down roots, and getting ready to be the next generation of shade, shelter, and beauty for the people and animals of our little neighborhood.

Have you seen pictures of Chernobyl now, nearly forty years after the nuclear meltdown flooded the place with radiation for miles?

Trees everywhere.

You and I: We are the new trees growing, while the dying oaks of consumerism, corruption, and scandal keep falling around us.

We don't have to wither just because *they* are diseased.

No, God is faithful. Wherever you are—in a bountiful forest or the rubble of a radiation zone—He will always be doing new things, planting new seeds, and bringing new life where we thought there was no hope.

It's my prayer that this book can help point you to fresh water.

There is so much beauty, depth, and wisdom in the songs, prayers, and practices of Christians throughout the centuries. I know I've only scratched the surface, but I invite you to explore more deeply anything here that "shimmers" to you.

Thank you for stepping out of the gift shop with me and daring to explore the wider world of this wild and incredible faith we're a part of.

Happy trails.

Dona Nobis Pacem.

Crown him the Son of God,
before the worlds began,
and ye who tread where he hath trod,
crown him the Son of Man;
who every grief hath known
that wrings the human breast,
and takes and bears them for His own,
that all in him may rest.

—"CROWN HIM WITH MANY CROWNS," MATTHEW BRIDGES, 1851

Thank You

TRILLIA NEWBELL: FOR YOUR INVITATION and belief in me as a first-time author. I hope I make you proud and don't get you in too much trouble.

Pam Pugh: for your gracious and merciful editing of this first-timer's book, and your patience, with his terrible, overuse, of the, comma,

Kevin and Wendy Twit: for all you've taught us—about hymns, theology, and Indelible Grace.

Dave and Donna Osenga, Mike and Carolyn Shipley, Cason Cooley, Paul Eckberg, Josh and Becca Wilson, Randall Goodgame: for listening and encouraging.

So many other friends who have helped make this possible in a million ways: David McCollum, Madison Frantz, Bryan Norman, Scott Sauls, Will and Kay Cook, John Delony, Rev. Kenny Benge, Rev. Andrew DeFusco, Ashley Cleveland, Mark Nicholas, Patrick Black, Laura McKenzie and the Church of the Redeemer family, Andrew Peterson, Dave Bruno, Pete Peterson and the Rabbit Room, Russ Ramsey, Nathan and Cassie Tasker and the Art House 2.0, Malcolm du Plessis, Jonathan Brown, Gilbert Nanlohy, Seth Talley, Matthew Smith, Jeremy Casella, Chris Weigel, Christopher Williams, The NFG, The Calvin Institute of Christian Worship for creating and maintaining Hymnary.org.

It's been the honor of a lifetime to work with and walk alongside so many wonderful artists, who have taught me so much that shaped this book: the Anchor Hymns crew, the Behold the Lamb Tour family, Sandra McCracken, Jess Ray, Taylor Leonhardt, Sarah Kroger, Leslie Jordan, Zach Bolen & Citizens, Tim Timmons, Paul Baloche, Matt Maher, Kat Davis, Brent Milligan, Ben Shive, Andy and Jill Gullahorn, Sara Groves, Jason Gray, Melanie Penn, The New Respects, the women of the Faithful Project, the In Every Generation team and community, The Normals, and Caedmon's Call, and so many others. Each chord and conversation is a gift.

To you reading this: the Kickstarter supporters, concert promoters, concert goers, record buyers, album streamers, Substack readers, podcast listeners, YouTube watchers, and all the other ways you engage, care for, and support me and other artists—Thank you!! Let's keep pushing the algorithms inch by inch to make this world a more kind and beautiful place.

To every YoungLife leader, youth group mentor, and Awana volunteer: Thanks for giving up countless hours with friends your own age to hang out with me and millions of other kids like me. (To you in those trenches now—some seeds grow more slowly than we can see. Take heart!)

To Alison, Ella, Sadie, and Charlotte: Thank you for supporting me and encouraging me. I'm the luckiest husband and dad in the world. It's the greatest gift of my life to get to walk these old, beautiful paths by your side. I love you dearly.

Notes

1. "Early In The Morning" copyright 2006, House of Mirrors Music, ASCAP, adm. by Integrated Rights.
2. "Hard to Get," words and music by Rich Mullins ©1998, Liturgy Legacy Music (adm. by WORD MUSIC/Word Music (a div. of Word Music).
3. Incidentally, to have these lyrics set to music, Chisholm sent them to his friend William Runyan, who was at that time employed by the Moody Bible Institute—the same company whose publishing arm, Moody Publishers, is publishing this book, 102 years later. How cool is that?
4. Charles Hutchinson Gabriel, *The Singers and Their Songs* (The Rodeheaver Company, 1916), 76.
5. Almost all new songs at the top of the CCLI chart (the chart that monitors what churches sing each week) are also big hits on Christian radio. In my work at record labels, and as an artist, I have been told many, many times over twenty-five years that core Christian words like "sin" will keep songs from getting played there, as they are neither positive nor encouraging.
6. Incidentally, this was basically the chorus of my first, and only, #1 Christian radio hit—that I wrote when I was 18 years old. I understand the heart of where this comes from.
7. William L. Andrews, *The Concise Oxford Companion to African American Literature* (Oxford University Press, 2001), 379; Edward Mikkelsen Jr., "Theophilus Gould Steward (1843–1924)," BlackPast.org., January 22, 2007, https://www.blackpast.org/african-american-history/steward-theophilus-gould-1843-1925/; T. G. Steward (Theophilus Gould), *From 1843 to 1924: Fifty Years in the Gospel Ministry: Twenty-Seven Years in the Pastorate; Sixteen Years' Active Service as Chaplain in the U.S. Army; Seven Years Professor in Wilberforce University; Two Trips to Europe; A Trip in Mexico* (A. M. E. Book Concern, 1921).
8. Josef A. Jungmann, *The Mass of the Roman Rite: Its Origins and Development*

(Benzinger Brothers, 1959), 18.
9. You can go to biblegateway.com and choose from many versions of Scripture. The examples here are from the New Internation Version, the New Revised Standard Version, The Voice, the New American Standard Bible, the Contemporary English Version, the New American Standard Bible 1995, and the New King James Version.
10. You can listen to this song at andrewosenga.com/anewlament.
11. Tess Schoonhoven, "Modern Hymn Writers, Keith and Kristyn Getty, Shape Worship Culture," *American Songwriter*, August 2, 2021, https://americansongwriter.com/modern-hymn-writers-keith-and-kristyn-getty-shape-worship-culture/.
12. James L. Crenshaw, *Education in Ancient Israel: Across the Deadening Silence* (Doubleday, 1998), 6.
13. Walter Brueggemann, *Awed to Heaven, Rooted in Earth* (Fortress Press, 2003).
14. *The Book of Common Prayer* (ACNA), (Anglican Liturgy Press, 2019), 130.
15. The Church of England, "B Penitence," https://www.churchofengland.org/prayer-and-worship/worship-texts-and-resources/common-worship/common-material/new-patterns-12.
16. *Book of Common Prayer*, 41.
17. *Book of Common Prayer*, 1928 edition, Order for Daily Evening Prayer.
18. The Church of England, *The Book of Common Prayer* (1662) (Cambridge University Press), https://www.churchofengland.org/prayer-and-worship/worship-texts-and-resources/common-worship/service-word/service-word-morning-and#ch6j.
19. See www.britannica.com/topic/Nicene-Creed and www.britannica.com/topic/Apostles-Creed.
20. Feel free to laugh.
21. Tim Hughes, "Here I Am to Worship," © 2001 Kingsway's Thankyou Music; adm. EMI Christian Music Publishing.
22. You can see the Icon of Christ Pantocrator at Andrewosenga.com/icon.
23. Kevin Twit, "Galatians 3:26-4:7 'The Status and The Experience of Adoption,'" Indelible Grace Music, https://igracemusic.com/rufsermons/Galatians%204a.pdf.
24. Raymond Studzinski, *Reading to Live: The Evolving Practice of Lectio Divina* (Liturgical Press, 2009), 52–53.
25. James C. Wilhoit and Evan B. Howard, *Discovering Lectio Divina: Bringing Scripture into Ordinary Life* (InterVarsity Press, 2012), 18–19.
26. Fr. Gregory Wassen, "The Divine Office—Its History and Development, The

Anglican Breviary, https://www.anglicanbreviary.net/the-divine-office.
27. Thomas McKenzie, *The Anglican Way* (Catherine, Inc., 2014), 113–23.
28. For example, https://www.wordonfire.org/pray/.
29. *The Spiritual Exercises of Saint Ignatius*, trans. George Ganss, S.J. (Loyola Press, 1992), 38.
30. You can actually see this in an early scene of the movie adaptation of *Blue Like Jazz*, in which our church was used as a set.
31. Kara Powell and Chap Clark, *Sticky Faith: Everyday Ideas to Build Lasting Faith in Your Kids* (Zondervan, 2011), 100–133.
32. "The State of Church Attendance: Trends and Statistics," ChurchTrac, https://www.churchtrac.com/articles/the-state-of-church-attendance-trends-and-statistics-2023.